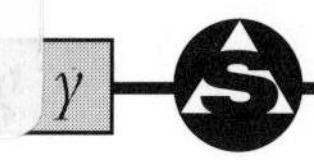

POWER *and* POLITICS

Ivor Morgan

Series Editor: Paul Selfe

Hodder & Stoughton
A MEMBER OF THE HODDER HEADLINE GROUP

DEDICATION

The book is dedicated to Carole, Joe, and Dan.

ACKNOWLEDGEMENTS

Paul Selfe provided thoughtful encouragement during the writing of this book.

Many thanks to sociology and politics students in Melbourne, Chippenham, Gainsborough, and Lincoln.

And thanks to R.S. Neale for his history class at Bath Technical College in 1963–64.

The publishers would like to thank the following for permission to reproduce copyright photographs: The Hutton Getty Picture Collection Ltd., p. 56, top, p. 82, top; PA News, p. 124, top.

Orders: please contact Bookpoint Ltd, 39 Milton Park, Abingdon, Oxon OX14 4TD.
Telephone: (44) 01235 400414, Fax: (44) 01235 400454. Lines are open from 9.00–6.00, Monday to Saturday, with a 24 hour message answering service.
Email address: orders@bookpoint.co.uk

A catalogue record for this title is available from The British Library

ISBN 0 340 74930X

First published 1999
Impression number 10 9 8 7 6 5 4 3 2 1
Year 2005 2004 2003 2002 2001 2000 1999

Cover photo from David King Collection

Typeset by Transet Limited, Coventry, England.
Printed in Great Britain for Hodder & Stoughton Educational, a division of Hodder Headline plc, 338 Euston Road, London NW1 3BH by Redwood Books, Trowbridge, Wilts.

CONTENTS

1

INTRODUCTION

HOW TO USE THE BOOK

EACH CHAPTER IN this book examines one or more of the central debates relating to the sociology of religion. The text is devised for readers with little or no background knowledge in the subject, and there are Study Points and Activities throughout to encourage a consideration of the issues raised. Student readers are advised to make use of these and answer them either on paper or in group discussion, a particularly fruitful way of learning; they will assist them to develop the skills of interpretation, analysis and evaluation. There are many ways of preparing for an exam, but a thorough understanding of the material is obviously crucial.

Each chapter is structured to give a clear understanding of the authors, concepts and issues that you need to know about. To assist understanding and facilitate later revision, it is often helpful to make concise notes.

MAKING NOTES FROM THE BOOK

Linear notes

- Bold headings establish key points: names, theories and concepts.
- Subheadings indicate details of relevant issues.
- A few numbered points list related arguments.

Diagram or pattern notes

- Use a large blank sheet of paper and write a key idea in the centre.
- Make links between this and related issues.
- Show also the connections between sub issues which share features in common.

Both systems have their advantages and disadvantages, and may take some time to perfect. Linear notes can be little more than a copy of what is already in the book and patterned notes can be confusing. But if you practise the skill, they can reduce material efficiently and concisely becoming invaluable for revision. Diagrammatic notes may be very useful for those with a strong visual memory and provide a clear overview of a whole issue, showing patterns of interconnection. The introduction of helpful drawings or a touch of humour into the format is often a good way to facilitate the recall of names, research studies and complex concepts.

Activity

- Make a diagram to show the two ways of making notes with their possible advantages and disadvantages

SKILLS ADVICE

Students must develop and display certain skills for their examination and recognise which ones are being tested in a question. The clues are frequently in key words in the opening part. The skill domains are:

1 **Knowledge and understanding:** the ability to discuss the views of the main theorists; their similarities and differences; the strengths and weaknesses of evidence. To gain marks students must display this when asked to *explain, examine, suggest a method, outline reasons.*
2 **Interpretation, application and analysis:** the use of evidence in a logical, relevant way, either to show how it supports arguments or refutes them. Students must show this ability when asked *identify, use items A/B/C, draw conclusions from a table.*
3 **Evaluation:** the skill of assessing evidence in a balanced way so that logical conclusions follow. Students can recognise this skill when asked to *assess, critically examine, comment on levels of reliability, compare and contrast*, or if asked *to what extent.*

Activity

Draw an evaluation table, as below, using the whole of an A4 page. Examine studies as you proceed in your work and fill in the relevant details. Keep it for revision purposes.

Sociologist		
Title of the study	Strengths	Weaknesses
Verdict		
Judgement/justification		

REVISION ADVICE

- Keep clear notes at all times in a file or on disk (with back up copy).
- Be familiar with exam papers and their demands.
- Become familiar with key authors, their theories, their research and sociological concepts.

Activity

Make and keep **Key Concept Cards**, as shown below.

COLLECTIVE CONSCIENCE

Key idea

A term used by **Durkheim** meaning:

- The existence of a social and moral order exterior to individuals and acting upon them as an independent force.
- The shared sentiments, beliefs and values of individuals which make up the **collective conscience.**
- In **traditional societies** it forms the basis of social order.
- As societies modernise the collective conscience weakens: **mechanical solidarity** is replaced by **organic solidarity**.

Key theorist: Emile Durkheim

Syllabus area: Sociological Theories of Religion: Functionalism

EXAMINATION ADVICE

To develop an effective method of writing, answers should be:

- **Sociological:** use the language and research findings of sociologists; do not use anecdotal opinion gathered from people not involved in sociology to support arguments.

- **Adequate in length:** enough is written to obtain the marks available.
- **Interconnected** with other parts of the syllabus (such as stratification, gender, ethnicity).
- **Logical:** the answer follows from the relevant evidence.
- **Balanced:** arguments and counter arguments are weighed; references are suitable.
- **Accurate:** reliable data is obtained from many sources.

The three skill areas on p 2 should be demonstrated, so that the question is answered effectively.

In displaying knowledge, the student is not necessarily also demonstrating interpretation.

- This must be specified with phrases like 'Therefore, this study leads to the view that…'
- Sections of answers should hang together, one leading to the next. This shows how the question is being answered by a process of analysis based on the evidence.
- Reach a conclusion based on the evidence used and the interpretations made.

The skill of evaluation is often regarded (not necessarily accurately) as the most problematic. Evaluation means being judge and jury; the strengths and weaknesses of evidence is assessed and an overall judgement about its value is made. To evaluate an argument or theory, consider whether it usefully opens up debate; explains the events studied; does it have major weaknesses?

Activity

Look through some past examination papers and pick out the evaluation questions. Underline the evaluation words and work out which skills are required.

COURSEWORK ADVICE

Coursework provides an opportunity to carry out a study using primary and/or secondary data to investigate an issue of sociological interest, and must address theoretical issues. The suggestions included at the end of each chapter may be adapted or used to generate further ideas. Final decision must be agreed with a teacher or tutor.

MAKING A PLAN

Before starting a piece of coursework, you should make a plan:

1. Read and make notes from articles describing research projects in journals.
2. Have a clear aim in mind; choose an issue that interests you and is within your ability.
3. Decide more precisely what you want to know; establish a simple hypothesis to test.
4. Select a range of possible methods; consider both quantitative and qualitative.
5. Decide on a range of possible sources of information.
6. List the people to whom you can seek help, perhaps including a statistician.

WRITING THE PROJECT

1. Seek frequent advice from a teacher or tutor.
2. Check the weighting for different objectives in the marking scheme.
3. Keep clear notes throughout, including new ideas and any problems that arise.
4. Limit its length (maximum 5,000 words).
5. Label and index the study in the following way:
   - a **Rationale:** a reason for choosing the subject; preliminary observations on the chosen area
   - b **Context:** an outline of the theoretical and empirical context of the study
   - c **Methodology:** a statement of the methodology used and reasons for selecting it
   - d **Content:** presentation of the evidence and/or argument including results
   - e **Evaluation:** the outcomes are weighed and strengths and weaknesses noted.
   - f **Sources:** all the sources of information are listed.

OR

- a **Title**
- b **Contents**
- c **Abstract:** a brief summary of the aims, methods, findings and evaluation.
- d **Rationale**
- e **The Study**
- f **Research Diary**
- g **Bibliography**
- h **Appendix:** to include proposal for the study, single examples of a questionnaire or other data-gathering instrument and transcripts of interviews.
- i **Annex:** to include raw data gathered.

Paul Selfe
Series editor

2

THE SOCIOLOGY OF POWER

Introduction

THIS CHAPTER LOOKS at theories and debates on the nature and distribution of power in society. Power can be used to exploit and dominate others or to further collective interests. It can be imposed through force or effected with consent. Pluralist theorists argue that power is dispersed amongst a large number of groups and ordinary citizens are able to influence the decision-making process. Elitist and Marxist theorists argue that power is concentrated in the hands of the few with ordinary citizens being denied any real say. Most analysis of power has concentrated on large macro-institutions such as the State, but power relationships also pervade the micro-politics of everyday life. Postmodernist theorists believe that disputes about knowledge and truth also involve a struggle for power.

DEFINING POWER

Bertrand Russell said power was a fundamental concept in social science. He defined power as 'the production of intended effects'. Russell noted that there is 'both power over human beings and power over dead matter' (1938).

- **Max Weber** saw 'the drive for power' as central to politics
- **Michael Mann** writes that 'in its most general sense, power is the ability to pursue and attain goals through mastery of one's environment' (1986).
- **Thomas Hobbes** focused on the 'dark side' of power: power as domination and the exploitation of others. He believed that human beings have 'a perpetual and restless desire of *power after power*, that ceaseth only in death'.

Table 1: *Theorists, concepts and issues in this chapter*

KEY THEORISTS	KEY CONCEPTS	KEY ISSUES
Hobbes, (1588–1679), Nietszche (1844–1900)	Power as domination over others	• Conflict view of power
Parsons (1902–79)	Power to achieve goals with others	• Consensus view of power
Mann (b. 1942), Giddens (b. 1938)	Distributive and collective power	• Power 'over' and power 'to'
Lukes (b. 1941)	Three dimensions of power	• Controlling the agenda of debate
Weber (1864–1920)	Power as authority	• Others consent to obey
Mills (1916–62)	Power as manipulation	• The powerful 'engineer' consent
Weber, Mills	Power as coercion	• The threat of force compels others to obey
Dahl (b. 1915)	Power in the hands of the many	• Pluralist analysis of power
Pareto (1842–1923), Marx (1818–83)	Power in the hands of the few	• Elitist and Marxist analysis of power
Weber, Althusser (1918–90)	Macro-physics of power	• The State as a key mechanism of power
Foucault (1926–84)	Micro-physics of power	• Power relationships embedded in everyday life
Baudrillard (b. 1929)	Post-modernist analysis	• Global communications and consumerism have changed the nature of power

He hoped that his readers 'will no longer suffer ambitious men through *the steams of your blood to wade to their own power'* (1651).

- **Friedrich Nietzsche** declared that 'This world is the will to power and nothing else besides'. All individuals crave power over others. As for those who talk of morality and compassion Nietzsche unmasked them as power seekers who simply use more subtle and cunning tactics that other people.
- **Anthony Giddens** defines power as 'the use of resources, of whatever kind, to secure outcomes'. Thus power consists of 'transformative capacity': 'the capability of human beings to intervene in a series of events so as to alter their course' (1977). According to his **structuration theory**, power structures have a dual character and are 'both enabling and constraining'. Power can be 'a medium for the realisation of collective human interests' as well as a means of controlling and oppressing others.

POWER AS COERCION AND POWER AS CONSENT

POWER AS A CONTINUUM

The classic sociological theorist of power is Max Weber. He defined power as 'the probability that one actor within a social relationship will be in a position to carry out his own will despite resistance...'. An 'actor' (an individual or an organisation) who controls the means of violence will be able to make others obey. Few people will argue with the barrel of a gun. Violence is an example of **coercive power**. People can be made to comply with one's will by making things unpleasant for them if they refuse. **C. Wright Mills** defined the powerful as 'those who are able to realise their will, even if others resist it'. (The powerful can also use their control over the flow of information to manipulate public opinion.) Other people can be made to do what one wants by **inducive power** (eg offering them rewards or 'bribes' of various kinds). Power can be based on coercive resources (eg the military); on **utilitarian** resources (eg economic possessions); and on **persuasive** resources (eg mass communications).

Amitai Etzioni sets out the following classification of the methods used by organisations to control their members:

1. *Coercive power* – the threat or application of physical sanctions.
2. *Remunerative or material power* – control over material resources and rewards.
3. *Symbolic or normative power* – the manipulation of moral status and prestige.

The types of involvement individuals have with organisations can be primarily **alienative** (eg prisons and concentration camps); **calculative** (business organisations); and **moral** (a church or a political party) (1961).

Michael Mann makes a classification of four sources of power:

1. Ideological power is derived from 'the human need to find ultimate meaning in life, to share norms and values, and to participate in aesthetic and ritual practices'.
2. Economic power is derived from 'the need to extract, transform, distribute and consume the resources of nature'.
3. Military power is derived from 'the social organisation of physical force'.
4. Political power is derived from 'the usefulness of territorial and centralised regulation' (1993).

The exercise of authority – institutionalised power – rests upon consent. People believe that those who issue commands possess **legitimacy** – that is they have a moral right to be obeyed. Power may have been gained through force, but the routinisation of obedience reduces the need to use force to secure compliance. **Nicolo Machiavelli**, the classic political theorist of the economy of violence, advised that when a new ruler seizes a state he 'ought to determine all the injuries that he will need to inflict. He should then inflict them once and for all, and in that way he will be able to set men's minds at rest and win them over to him when he confers benefits' (1524).

Max Weber distinguished between three types of authority:

1 **charismatic authority**: individuals are obeyed because they are seen as possessing 'supernatural, superhuman, or at least specifically exceptional powers or qualities'.
2 **traditional authority**: this rests on 'an established belief in the sanctity of immemorial traditions'.
3 **rational-legal authority**: this rests on 'belief in the legality of a consciously created order'. It consists of obedience towards a set of impartially applied rules which are universalistic (they apply to everyone) and administered impersonally.

Modern States are based on rational-legal authority structures. Thus at one extreme of the coercion–consent continuum of power is force and violence: individuals are compelled to obey or be killed, imprisoned, tortured etc. In the middle are **influence** – individuals are persuaded to change their minds – and **manipulation** – individuals are cynically deceived. At the other extreme is legitimacy and consent: individuals voluntarily and freely choose to obey those who hold positions of authority.

ZERO SUM AND VARIABLE SUM CONCEPTS OF POWER

Conflict theorists favour a zero sum view of power: the size of the 'power cake' is fixed so that more power for one group means less power for another. Gains by X mean losses for Y. Mann refers to this as **distributive power**.

Consensus theorists favour a variable sum view of power: the size of the 'power cake' can vary and will expand if individuals pool their efforts. If X and Y work together rather than against each other they will both gain more power. Mann refers to this as **collective power**.

The functionalist **Talcott Parsons** defined power in terms of using resources to achieve shared objectives. If individuals have confidence in the political system 'power inflation' takes place and society's effectiveness in achieving its goals will be increased. (Too much dwelling on the zero-sum dimension of power could lower confidence in the political system and bring about 'power deflation'!)

President Kennedy put forward a 'functionalist' view when he declared: 'By working together we have recognised that a rising tide lifts all the boats.'

POINTS OF EVALUATION

1 Parsons' critics see him as giving a conservative justification of the status quo. The fact that the powerful may further their own interests at the expense of the collective good is ignored. But as Giddens notes: 'positions of power offer to their incumbents definite material and psychological rewards, and thereby stimulate conflicts between those who want power and those who have it'.
2 The focus of consensus theory is on power to achieve shared goals. The proponents of this view emphasise how power can be used for collective purposes to the benefit of society at large. The focus of conflict theory is on power to achieve sectional goals. The advocates of this view emphasise how power can be used for distributive purposes to the benefit of particular groups.

Study point

Think of three examples of power being used:
1 as a means of achieving domination **over** others;
2 as a means **to** further the collective good.

Activity

Divide into two groups.
1 One groups advocates consensus theory. Consider arguments for instituting a school or college council which includes staff and students.
2 One group advocates conflict theory. Consider arguments which might be used to oppose a student/staff council.

THE DISTRIBUTION OF POWER

Pluralists argue that power is shared amongst a wide variety of groups. (Pluralists are sometimes referred to as functionalist–pluralists, although pluralists place less emphasis on value-consensus than functionalists.) Pluralist though has been influenced by the classic concept of the **separation of powers**. This was put forward by **Baron Montesquieu** in *The Spirit of the Laws* (1748). He argued that:

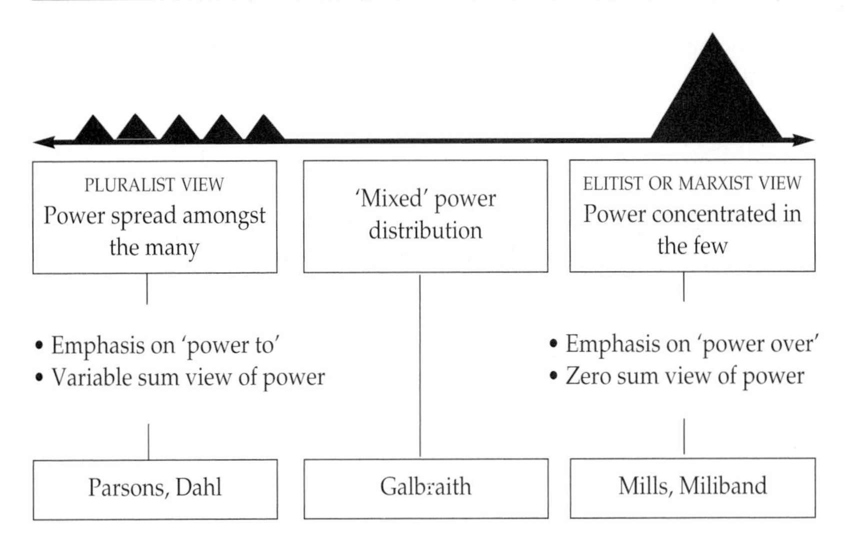

THEORIES OF POWER DISTRIBUTION

- Liberty depends on no single group being able to gain control of all the key institutions of political power.
- Consequently the **executive** (government), **legislature** (parliament), and **judiciary** (the courts) must be in the hands of different individuals.

Pluralists believe that the institutions of representative democracy give ordinary citizens a say in decision-making. The influence of elite groups is confined to specific policy areas. Power is 'non-cumulative' – groups with access to government on some issues are ignored on others. So, if the general secretary of the British Medical Association 'attempted to intervene in the fixing of intervention prices for dairy products, he might be deemed to require help from members of his profession practising psychiatric medicine' (**Grant**, 1989).

Interactionists focus on the rewards which individuals derive from obeying commands and conforming to the dictates of authority structures. **Peter Blau** refers to 'socialised morality': individuals feel a sense of moral obligation to support structures which have conferred benefits and privileges on them (1974).

'Mixed' power theorists (such as the Canadian-born US economist **J.K. Galbraith** have put forward the concept of **countervailing power**.

- The power of employers is countered by the power of trade unions.
- The power of business corporations is countered by the state (through regulatory bodies, taxation and law).

- A concentration of power in one sector of society can lead to the formation of a rival power centre in another sector of society.

Marxists argue that power is concentrated in the hands of a ruling class which uses the State to protect and advance its economic interests. In the view of the French neo-marxist **Louis Althusser** the State has a dual structure: one 'arm' is the **Ideological State Apparatus** (ISA) (which includes the mass media and schools); the other 'arm' is the **Repressive State Apparatus** (RSA) (which includes the police and the army) (1971). The Italian neo-marxist **Antonio Gramsci** argued that a successful ruling class exercises **hegemony** – cultural leadership – over the population and its ideology comes to be accepted as part of the 'common sense of the epoch'. **Elitist** theorists see power as concentrated in the hands of well organised minorities. Classical elitists such as **Vilfredo Pareto** and **Gaetano Mosca** celebrated elite domination and saw it as both inevitable and desirable. In Mosca's view capacity for organisation is a key to elite rule. 'The minority is organised for the very reason it is a minority.'

- The powerful manipulate the consent of the masses by inventing a 'political formula' (or ideology) which justifies their rule, for example the doctrine of the divine right of kings.
- Elections are essentially the process by which a member of the political elite 'has himself elected by the voters'.

Democratic elitists such as **Joseph Schumpeter** see participatory democracy as impractical: ordinary people lack the time and expertise to take part in complex decision-making. However periodic elections compel political elites to engage in 'a competitive struggle for the people's vote'. In totalitarian States – where only one party is permitted – a single elite retains a permanent hold on power. In democratic States a number of parties compete for public support, and people have the power to remove an unpopular party from office. **John Dunn** writes: 'To be given the opportunity to choose at intervals between candidates for rule is not much. But it can readily become a pronounced improvement on never being given that opportunity.'

POINTS OF EVALUATION

1. Theories of the distribution of power reflect different ideological positions.
2. Pluralists have a broadly positive view of democracy in the United Kingdom and claim that power is dispersed amongst a variety of groups.
3. Marxists have a critical view of democracy in the UK and claim that power is concentrated in the hands of the few.
4. Elitists claim that power in all societies is concentrated in the hands of the few.

THE MICRO-PHYSICS OF POWER

A distinction has been drawn between **Politics 1** and **Politics 2**. The focus of Politics 2 is on 'the specialised machinery of government together with the administrative apparatus of State and Party organisation'. The focus of Politics 1 is on the power relationships of everyday life. In fact, 'the exercise of constraint in any relationship' is 'political' (**Peter Worsley**, 1977). **Marvin E. Olsen** (1970) notes that 'if by social interaction we mean one actor affecting another, then every instance of interaction and every social relationship involves the exercise of power'. Mann distinguishes between **authoritative power** which 'is actually willed by groups and institutions' and **diffused power** which is 'not directly commanded; it spreads in a relatively spontaneous, unconscious, and decentred way'. The term the micro-physics of power was coined by **Michel Foucault**. (The macro-physics of power focuses on large-scale institutions such as the State.)

- In Foucault's view the State 'is far from being able to occupy the whole field of actual power relations'. Power for Foucault is 'microcellular', and power relationships are found in all areas of social life including 'the body, sexuality, the family, kinship, knowledge, technology, and so forth'. It involves not only physical control over objects and spaces but also struggles over 'discourse' (language and communication) and the imposition of particular definitions of knowledge and truth. 'Power produces knowledge' as well as armies and weapons.
- For the postmodernist theorist **Jean-Francois Lyotard** 'knowledge and power are simply two sides of the same question: who decides what knowledge is, and who knows what needs to be decided?' (1984).

LEADING THEORISTS

'POWER IS IN THE HANDS OF THE MANY'

Robert Dahl sees the claim that power is concentrated in the hands of a ruling elite as resting on three key assumptions:

1. The hypothetical ruling elite is a well defined group.
2. There is a fair sample of cases involving key political decisions in which the preferences of the hypothetical elite run counter to any other likely group.
3. In such cases the preferences of the elite regularly prevail.

His empirical (that is practical and factual) study of the Eastern USA city of New Haven convinced Dahl that each of these assumptions was flawed. No single elite dominated decision-making, regular elections ensured that every section of the population had some political influence, and the city's power structure was pluralistic: 'New Haven is a republic of unequal citizens, but for all that a republic' (1961).

- **Arnold Rose** studied the USA power structure (1967) and put forward a pluralistic **multiple-elite hypothesis**. Like Dahl he argued that power in the USA is shared amongst 'many elites, each relatively small numerically and operating in different spheres of life'.
- **Suzanne Keller** believes that in earlier periods of history it was indeed possible for a single dominant elite to organise all the leadership functions in society. But growth in population, in bureaucratic administration, and the emergence of a highly complex economy has led to a dispersal of power. Today decision-making has to be shared between the various political, economic, military, scientific, moral and cultural elites which possess the specialised professional skills needed to keep society afloat (1968).
- **Christopher Hewitt** focused on specific policy areas in postwar British politics. He then analysed major decisions to see if a single elite had been able to get its way. Elites were found to be divided amongst themselves. Thus the introduction of commercial television in 1954 was favoured by some groups (such as advertising companies) but opposed by others (such as newspaper and cinema interests). Hewitt concluded that policy-making 'does not appear to be "elitist" in the sense that any single elite is dominant. Instead the picture of national power that is revealed suggests a "pluralist" interpretation since a diversity of conflicting interests are involved in many issues, without any one interest being consistently successful in realising its goals' (1974).

'POWER IS IN THE HANDS OF THE FEW'

- **Floyd Hunter** used a **reputational approach** in his study of 'Regional City' (1953). Interviews with well known 'prominent persons' provided him with a list of 27 individuals who were seen as belonging to the city's power elite. These names were then reduced to a list of ten 'top leaders'. He claimed that power in 'Regional City' – unlike 'New Haven' – was concentrated in the hands of a small business-dominated elite.
- **G. William Domhoff** claims that the USA is dominated by an upper class – a class 'which receives a disproportionate amount of the country's income, owns a disproportionate amount of the country's wealth and contributes a disproportionate number of its members to the controlling institutions and key decision-making groups in that country'. Shared educational backgrounds, membership of the same prestigious clubs, intermarriage, and common summer resort residential patterns reinforce the social cohesion and the unity of the ruling class (1967).
- The neo-marxist **Nicos Poulantzas** argues that structural factors – the dynamics of the class system – determine the distribution of power. The social origins of members of the political elite have little influence on State policy.

Even 'if all of the bourgeoisie were to become workers and vice versa, or any similar wholesale movement between classes took place, the class structure of the capitalist formation would not change in any fundamental way. The places of capital, of the working class, and of the petty bourgeoisie would still be there' (1978).

- The neo-marxist **Ralph Miliband** accepts that there are elements of pluralism in the UK power structure and that different elite groups compete with each other for influence. But he believes that such 'elite pluralism' does not 'prevent the separate elites in capitalist society from constituting a dominant economic class, possessed of a high degree of cohesion and solidarity, with common interests and common purposes which far transcend their specific differences and disagreements'. In fact, the power exerted by business is such that it would be 'extremely *difficult* for governments to impose upon it policies to which it is firmly opposed' (1969).
- **John Scott** prefers the term **power bloc** to ruling class. Business has a dominant position in terms of the exercise of State power, but it cannot run the whole show on its own. It has to win support and form alliances with other social groups such as the entrepreneurial middle class and top managers and professionals (1991).

Study point

Empirical studies of community power structures (such as 'New Haven' and 'Regional City') have been criticised for assuming that the power structure of a city is a microcosm of the power structure of the nation. The *national* power structure could be elitist even though *city* power structures are pluralistic, or vice versa. How valid is it to draw generalisations about the national distribution of power from investigations of community power structures?

IMAGES OF POWER PERVADE EVERYDAY LIFE

POSTMODERNISM

Postmodernists have provided new perspectives on the nature of power.

- Foucault argues that relationships of domination and resistance are woven into the fabric of everyday life. New forms of **disciplinary power** were developed in the eighteenth century and the human body was subjected to systematic inspection, monitoring, and surveillance. The aim of the 'bio-politics' was to turn the body into an efficient machine and integrate it into the routines of institutions such as the army, the school, and the factory (1984).

- **Jean Baudrillard** claims that media saturation and 'hyperreality' are dominant features of contemporary society: power has been transformed into a sign, an image, and it is no longer possible to distinguish fact from illusion, the real from the represented. Power 'is no longer an objective, locatable process' (1987).
- **Guy Debord** declared: 'All that was once directly lived has become mere representation... In a world that has *really* been turned on its head, truth is a moment of falsehood (1967).

POINTS OF EVALUATION

1. Critics of Dahl's empirical approach see it as ignoring the 'hidden dimension' of decision-making: the powerful may be able to shape the agenda of public debate.
2. Critics of Keller point out that there are examples of highly complex modern societies (eg Nazi Germany) in which enormous power *was* concentrated in the hands of a single leadership elite.

NAZI GERMANY IS AN EXAMPLE OF A COMPLEX SOCIETY IN WHICH POWER WAS CONCENTRATED INTO THE HANDS OF A SINGLE LEADERSHIP ELITE

3 Critics of Miliband and Domhoff see them as ignoring the depth of divisions which exist within the dominant class, and the ways in which democratic institutions can work to safeguard the public interest.
4 Critics of postmodernist approaches argue that if power is redefined as pervading all modes of thought and every social relationship – if power is seen as being everywhere – it ends up being nowhere. As **Eagleton** puts it: 'Any word which covers everything loses its cutting edge and dwindles to any empty sound.' (For some penetrating criticisms of postmodernism see Daniel Morgan, Coursework, *Sociology Review*, November 1998.)
5 Ideological awareness is important when one evaluates the views of rival theorists. As a rule, radical critics of the status quo discover (surprise, surprise) that power is exercised *against* the public interest, while conservative supporters of the status quo discover (surprise, surprise) that power is exercised *in* the public interest.

STEVEN LUKES – A RADICAL VIEW (1974)

Lukes identifies the following *three dimensions of power*:

1 *Success in the decision-making process* – a group has clear preferences on a number of specific issues and is regularly able to get its way.
2 *Setting the decision-making agenda* – a group is able to prevent policies it dislikes from being debated. The political system favours the powerful and the policy preferences of the powerless are ignored. The powerful are able to keep a whole range of potential issues off the agenda: they become 'non-decisions'.
3 *Shaping the preferences of others* – a group is able to achieve this 'through the control of information, through the mass media and through the processes of socialisation'. The powerful are able to manipulate the beliefs of the powerless whose own 'real interests' are not even articulated.

POINTS OF EVALUATION

1 How can it be known that people's 'real interests' are being ignored if they do not express what these are?
2 Pluralists see the mass media as reflecting a wide variety of viewpoints rather than being controlled by the powerful.
3 From time to time governments implement policies which have been vigorously opposed by the powerful.

Activity

1 Make a list of three policy issues which are currently on the public decision-making agenda and are being debated in Parliament.
2 Make a list of three potential policy issues which are *not* on the public decision-making agenda and are *not* being debated in Parliament.
3 Examine the view that the three potential policy issues you have named in question 2 above are not on the public decision-making agenda because of manipulation of the powerless by the powerful.

Study point

The following quotations are from pluralist, Marxist, and elitist, theorists of the distribution of power. Which is which?

1 *'The top of modern American society is increasingly unified, and often seems wilfully co-ordinated: at the top there has emerged an elite whose power probably exceeds that of any small group of men in world history. The middle levels are often a drifting set of stalemated forces... The bottom of this society is politically fragmented, and, even as a passive fact, increasingly powerless...'*

2 *'There exists in Britain a "ruling class" if we mean by it a group which provides the majority of those who occupy positions of power and who, in their turn, can materially assist* their *sons to reach similar positions.'*

3 *'No secret cabal controls politics... (power) is specialised, with individuals who are influential in one sector tending not to be influential in another.'*

Answers on p. 135.

WEALTH CONCENTRATION AND THE EXERCISE OF POWER

In the UK, a high proportion of wealth is concentrated in the hands of a small minority of the population. According to Peter Worsley this provides evidence for the existence of a dominant class which is powerful enough to safeguard its economic privileges. **David Lockwood** disagrees and argues that the existence of economic inequality does not in itself provide evidence for the existence of a powerful dominant class. It has also to be shown that inequality is 'in large part a product of managed consensus, or manipulation...' (1973).

Activity

In small groups discuss whether the concentration of large-scale wealth ownership is:

1 an indication of the power of the dominant class and its capacity to protect its vital economic interests;
2 a result – not of a calculated political strategy – but of the operation of impersonal market forces; or
3 an indication of a social consensus (ie widespread agreement) that economic inequality is desirable and brings with it more advantages than disadvantages.

SUMMARY

- The 'transformative capacity' of power can be used:
  1 to dominate and oppress others
  2 to promote collective human interests.
- Key sources of power include ideological, economic, military, and political power.
- The exercise of legitimate authority rests upon voluntary consent. The Weberian classification of authority distinguishes between charismatic, traditional, and rational-legal forms of authority.
- Theorists who view society as characterised by a consensus of shared values favour a variable sum concept of power. Theorists who view society as characterised by conflict between antagonistic groups favour a zero sum concept of power.
- In the pluralist analysis power is dispersed amongst numerous groups in society. In the Marxist analysis power is concentrated in the hands of a ruling class which owns the means of production. In the elitist analysis power is concentrated in the hands of well organised minorities.
- The macro-physics of power (Politics 2) studies the impact of decisions taken by large-scale institutions, such as the State. The micro-physics of power (Politics 1) studies the exercise of power in everyday social relationships. For postmodernist theorists knowledge and ideas are sites of the struggle for power.
- Power concentration theorists have put forward concepts of power elite; governing elite; ruling class; power bloc.
- Pluralist theorists have put forward concepts of the separation of power; multiple-elites; strategic elites; polyarchal democracy.
- Postmodernist theorists have put forward the concept of 'hyperreality' – signs and images which define reality. In industrial society new forms of disciplinary power have emerged which are based on surveillance and 'bio-politics' of control of the body.

Group work

Divide into groups and discuss the following two issues. Then devise a presentation using photographs from the press; sound clips from news items; video clips; information from interviews and questionnaires. Draw conclusions.

1 Friedrich Nietzsche's claim that all individuals are motivated by a will to power.
2 The view that power relationships of domination and resistance are evident in everyday social interaction, for example in gender relationships.

Practice Questions

1 '"Ruling class" is a badly loaded phrase. "Class" is an economic term; "rule" is a political one. The phrase "ruling class" thus contains the theory that an economic class rules politically.' (C. Wright Mills). Explain and discuss.
2 Examine the view that power in Britain is shared amongst a large number of groups with the State acting as a neutral referee in deciding on their claims.
3 'Pluralists provide only a partial perspective... They assume that people will automatically participate in politics if their interests are threatened; and they assume that all interests possess the "potential" to organise and be influential in politics.' From John Dearlove and Peter Saunders in *Introduction to British Politics* (1991). Discuss.

Coursework

1 Research individuals' perceptions of the UK power structure. Is the dominant view one of a power structure which ordinary citizens can influence, or of a power structure which is controlled by a dominant elite or ruling class?
2 Carry out a case study of the power structure of an organisation with which you are familiar (eg an educational institution). Analyse the methods which are used to control individuals and keep them 'in line'. Assess how effective these are.
3 Investigate the power structure of your local community. Use a 'reputational approach': interview key individuals in business, politics, and the media and ask them to name the 'leaders who count' in the area.

3

THE STATE AND DEMOCRACY

Introduction

THIS CHAPTER EXAMINES the concept of the State and the nature of democracy. The State is an organisation which exercises control over a specific territory. It is a focal point for the struggle for power. The modern State was developed in Western Europe some four centuries ago. Today almost the entire land surface of the planet is subjected to State control. The totalitarian State is based on a one-party dictatorship and uses modern technology to impose a single ideology. In the pluralist State regular elections take place, numerous groups influence the decision-making process, and a wide variety of political views are expressed. The idea of democracy was first developed in the city-state of ancient Athens. Democracy in the United Kingdom is based on indirect or representative democracy rather than on direct democracy. Before 1832 only wealthy male landowners were able to vote. Today (with a few exceptions) all adult citizens can vote. There is a continuing debate on how democratic participation can be extended.

THE STATE

MAX WEBER

The classic theorist of the State is Max Weber. Weber defined the State in terms of the *means* it employs to maintain power – that is, the use of force. 'A compulsory political association with continuous organisation will be called a "State" if and in so far as its administrative staff successfully upholds a claim to the *monopoly* of the *legitimate* use of physical force in the enforcement of its order.'

Table 2: *Theorists, concepts and issues in this chapter*

Key Theorists	Key concepts	Key issues
Weber (1864–1920)	The State	• Monopoly of the legitimate use of force
Bodin (1529–96)	Sovereignty	• Supreme power
Friedrich and Brzezinski (b. 1928)	Totalitarian State	• Total control of the population
Pahl and Winkler	Corporate State	• Functional groups involved in policy-making
Mills (1916–62)	Power elite State	• Key elites take major policy decisions
Offe, Poulantzas (1936–79), Miliband	Capitalist State	• Ruling class shapes policy decisions
Djilas (1911–95)	New class State	• Political bureaucracy shapes policy decisions
Dahl (b. 1915)	Pluralist State	• Plurality of groups shape policy decisions
Pericles (c. 490–429 BC)	Democracy	• Power is exercised by the people
Rousseau (1712–78)	Direct democracy	• Citizens debate and legislate
Burke (1729–97)	Indirect democracy	• Elected representatives debate and legislate on citizens' behalf

According to Weber 'all political formations are formations of violence' and the State is the 'last source of all legitimate physical violence'. Thus the State holds a monopoly of the legitimate use of force within a given territory. In Weber's view, national and international politics are dominated by a struggle for power. In 1894 in his *Inaugural Lecture* at Freiburg University, he warned people against deluding themselves 'that peace and happiness are hidden in the lap of the future; on the contrary, only in a hard struggle between man and man can elbow room be won in our earthly existence'.

Weber took a conservative nationalist position in politics. Shortly after the outbreak of the 1914–18 First World War, he declared that the war – despite 'all its ugliness' – was 'great and wonderful'. In his view the world's 'power-states' were locked in a struggle for political domination.

Weber's analysis had a major influence on functionalist theory:

- Talcott Parsons locates the State within the political sub-system. It formulates aims and objectives for the social system and fulfils the **goal-attainment** function.

- Antonio Gramsci defined the State as 'hegemony protected by armoured coercion'.
- Louis Althusser distinguished between the Ideological State Apparatus and the Repressive State Apparatus (see page 12). Both Gramsci and Althusser analyse State power in terms of a mix of consent and force.

THE HISTORY OF THE STATE

Archaeological findings reveal that States – organisations with a monopoly of violence over a specific territory – have existed since around 6000 BC. During the sixteenth and seventeenth centuries in Western Europe a number of **absolutist** States were formed. These proceeded to:

- centralise power
- set up bureaucracies and permanent armies
- establish systems of taxation and single currencies

Over the last two centuries there has been a ten-fold increase in the number of States. Apart from Antarctica, the entire planet is now divided into States. One hundred and eighty-five States were represented in the United Nations in 1998.

Sovereignty

The concept of sovereignty refers to the exclusive right to make law and exercise power over a specific territory.

The doctrine of sovereignty was first formulated by the French legal theorist **Jean Bodin**. It holds that the authority of a sovereign State cannot be overruled by a higher body. In the seventeenth century the doctrine of **parliamentary sovereignty** was developed: no higher body can override the authority of the national parliament. However, the establishment of new supra-national institutions (such as the European Union which dates from the 1958 Treaty of Rome) has generated new debates about the nature of sovereignty.

In jurisprudence (the philosophy of law) a distinction is made between ***de facto*** power (something which exists in fact, whether or not it is 'right') and ***de jure*** (or 'rightful') authority. A number of States claim *de jure* authority but lack the *de facto* power to enforce their commands.

Study point

Would you favour giving up British sovereignty over territory (say, a remote island) rather than going to war to defend it?

Terms associated with the State

'Civil society' refers to voluntary and private organisations which are outside control of the State. The term 'State' refers to the permanent institutions which exercise authority over a specific territory (eg the civil service, the military, the judiciary, the police, local government, Parliament). The United Kingdom of Great Britain is a multinational State (comprised of England, Scotland, Wales and Northern Ireland). The 'government' is composed of ministers who are members of either the House of Commons or the House of Lords. Senior ministers are members of the 'cabinet'. The cabinet meets once a week and discusses government policy. Junior members of the government are not members of the cabinet, but – like cabinet ministers – they are expected to publicly support government policy. While governments come and go, the institutions of the State endure.

Activity

1. Study the international news sections of some 'quality' newspapers. Find examples of States which are unable to exercise *de facto* power over parts of the national territory. In small groups compile a list of factors which can lead to a loss of *de facto* power.
2. Find the names of five government ministers who are members of the cabinet and the names of five ministers who are not in the cabinet.
3. Which three posts in the cabinet (other than that held by the Prime Minister) are likely to carry the greatest power?

Study point

Information on the cabinet, government departments, and government policy is available on the following web sites:

- CCTA Government Information Service: http://www.open.gov.uk
- No. 10 Downing Street: http://www.number-10.gov.uk/index.html
- Hansard (House of Commons reports): http://www.parliament.the-stationery-office.co.uk

THEORIES OF THE STATE

THE TOTALITARIAN STATE

In a totalitarian State the population is under the total control of a single party. Modern technology (such as the mass media) is used to mobilise support for the official ideology. Police terror silences dissent. Examples of totalitarian States include Nazi Germany (1933–45) and Stalinist Russia (1928–53). All totalitarian States are dictatorships: power is exercised in an arbitrary way and is unrestricted by law. But not all dictatorships are totalitarian. The population is not mobilised to support the official ideology in a non-totalitarian dictatorship. The majority of totalitarian States are **autocracies**: one person within the ruling party wields absolute power.

POINTS OF EVALUATION

1 *Total* control of the population is impossible to achieve. Even in Hitler's Germany and Stalin's Russia there were pockets of resistance.
2 Ancient Sparta has been described as 'totalitarian'. In small-scale societies the population can be indoctrinated and controlled without using modern technology.

Study point

Find an example of a non-totalitarian dictatorship.

THE CORPORATE STATE

Within a corporate State the interests of key functional groups (such as large business corporations) are represented in a corporative chamber. The elected Parliament is either stripped of its authority or abolished altogether.

- Corporatist ideology was a feature of the Fascist State established in Italy in 1922 by **Mussolini**. Mussolini viewed society as an integrated organism in which 'every interest and every individual is subordinated to the overriding purpose of the nation'.
- In the UK during the 1960s and 1970s there was a shift towards **neo-** or **liberal corporatism**. The National Economic Development Council (NEDC, known as 'Neddy', founded in 1961 by Macmillan's Conservative Government) was a forum for regular tripartite meetings between representatives of business, unions, and government. State intervention and economic planning increased

under both the 1970–74 Conservative Government of Heath and the 1974–79 Labour Governments of Wilson and Callaghan. Leading pressure groups were partially incorporated into the governing process.

- **R. E. Pahl** and **J. T. Winkler** saw the British State of this period as engaged in a neo-corporatist project to build a 'comprehensive economic system' and construct a more unified and integrated social order (1974). Reversing the apparent shift towards corporatism was an important ideological theme of Margaret Thatcher's 1979 election campaign.

POINTS OF EVALUATION

1 In Mussolini's Italy power was concentrated in leadership of the Fascist State rather than in the corporative chamber.
2 In the UK in the 1970s neither the Confederation of British Industry (CBI) or the Trade Union Congress (TUC) had the power to compel their members to comply with agreements made with government. Parliament continued to represent public opinion, whereas 'the corporativist scenario leaves no room for any other kind of representation except functional representation through economic function' (**McCelland**, 1996).

Study point

Give an example of two types of ideology which are sharply opposed to each other.

THE POWER ELITE STATE

According to radical elite theorists such as C. Wright Mills politics in the USA is now dominated by a power elite. He defined this as 'those political, economic and military circles which, as an intricate set of overlapping cliques, share decisions having at least national consequences'. In Mills' view the intellectual calibre of the individuals at the centre of this new 'triangle of power' is itself a cause for concern: 'George Washington in 1783 relaxed with Voltaire's *Letters* and Locke's *On Human Understanding*; Eisenhower read cowboy tales and detective stories' (1956).

POINTS OF EVALUATION

Vilfredo Pareto and other classical elite theorists view history as a 'graveyard of aristocracies' with one elite being overthrown and replaced by another – which in time will itself be overthrown. In *Mind and Society* (1916) Pareto claimed that *all* societies are divided between the mass of the population – the non-elite – and the elite – those who have the greatest ability. The elite consists of two sections: the non-governing elite and the governing elite, 'a smaller, choicer class that effectively exercises control'. Revolutions occur but these do not signify an end to elite domination. 'From time to time sudden and violent disturbances occur. There is a flood – the river overflows its banks. Afterwards, the new governing elite again resumes.' As for the belief that power can be democratically exercised by the people and not by an exploitative elite this, in Pareto's view, is simply a naive illusion.

Study point

Suggest two criticisms of Pareto's arguments.

THE CAPITALIST STATE

In the view of **Claus Offe** this type of State has four key characteristics:

1 Production and control of the means of production is in private hands.
2 Governments are dependent on taxation revenue.
3 It is in the self-interest of the State to encourage a healthy private sector.
4 To gain control of the State, a group has to win an election and gain democratic legitimation (1984).

POINTS OF EVALUATION

1 For Nicos Poulantzas one of the key roles of the State is to facilitate the growth and expansion of the economy and maximise the long-term profitability of capital. According to his **structuralist** analysis it is objective and external factors – not the subjective intentions of individual politicians – which determine government policy. The higher the proportion of cabinet ministers who come from a non-business background the better: 'The capitalist state best serves the interest of the capitalist state only when members of this class do not participate directly in the state apparatus, that is to say when the *ruling class* is not the *politically governing class* (1969).
2 Ralph Miliband puts forward an instrumentalist analysis of the State. Civil servants and government ministers use the State as an instrument to advance their own economic interests. Non-structural factors – the aims and intentions of members of the political elite – *do* have an influence on policy. Policy is not simply determined by impersonal structural forces and the imperatives of profit.

Study point

Distinguish between structuralist and non-structuralist factors. Give examples of each.

Activity

- Cabinet A consists of 23 individuals who come from an overwhelmingly upper-middle class, public school, Oxbridge social background.
- Cabinet B consists of 23 individuals who come from an overwhelmingly working class, state school social background.

In small groups discuss whether the policies pursued by Cabinet A will be likely to differ significantly from the policies pursued by Cabinet B. What influence (if any) does the social composition of the political elite have on decision-making?

THE NEW CLASS STATE

Milovan Djilas (a former vice-president of the ex-communist State of Yugoslavia) claims that a **new class** of Party officials and top administrators exerts a major influence on policy-making in communist States.

- In communist States members of the **political bureaucracy** have privileged lifestyles.
- These privileges are passed on (by way of 'connections' rather than private property) to children, who attend elite schools and universities and use 'blat' or nepotism (favouritism by relatives and family friends) to obtain high status employment.
- The new class consists of those who have 'special privileges and economic preference because of the administrative monopoly they hold' (1957).

POINTS OF EVALUATION

1 **Leon Trotsky** viewed the Soviet Union as a **degenerate workers' state** – a half-way house between capitalism and socialism. He rejected the view that the bureaucracy was a class (new or old) on the grounds that it did not own private property and capital (1936).
2 **Robert Michels**, a classical elite theorist, predicted that a communist revolution would lead to power passing into the hands of an oligarchy. His book *Political Parties. A Sociological Study of the Oligarchical Tendencies of*

Modern Democracy (1911) was based on a study of the power structure of the German Social Democratic Party. In theory, the Party was committed to participatory democracy and maximising the involvement of ordinary party members. But in practice an **Iron Law of Oligarchy** ensured that the Party was controlled by a small elite of full-time organisers and leaders who acquired organisational expertise, controlled by Party's finances and network of communications, enjoyed their status and embourgeoisified lifestyles, and were treated in a deferential way by ordinary party members. Revolutionary communists said, 'To make a revolution we need organisation.' Michels' response was 'Who says organisation says oligarchy.' In his view organisation equals rule by an oligarchy equals betrayal of the working class.

THE PLURALIST STATE

Dahl argues that in deciding on the claims of rival groups the State acts as a neutral umpire and safeguards the public interest. Regular elections, the accountability of government to parliament, the force of public opinion, the scrutiny of the powerful by the mass media, competition between political parties – these processes ensure that no single class, elite or section of society is able to exert control over the policy-making process. Even the interests of apathetic and unorganised groups of the population have to be taken into account by governments. Otherwise they risk being voted out of office at the next election. Individuals have numerous cross-cutting ties – they support X on one issue but oppose X on another. This reduces the possibility of any single group acquiring too much power.

The decision-making process is shaped by multiple influences. (A study in Birmingham found that over 4,000 pressure groups actively sought to influence decision-making in the city.) There is a large political class (made up of commentors, journalists, party and pressure group activists) which continually monitors every aspect of government activity. The supposedly 'all-powerful' President of the USA cannot even ensure that his intimate actions in private rooms in the White House are kept hidden from the public gaze! Societies like the USA and the UK are polyarchal democracies in which the many (poly) rule (archo).

POINTS OF EVALUATION

1 C. Wright Mills' theory of power being concentrated in the hands of a single elite is over-conspiratorial.
2 The pluralist State promotes the illusion of political freedom, but in a crisis situation it reveals its true dictatorial colours. During the miners' strike of 1984–5 roads were blocked in order to prevent supporters of the National Union of Miners travelling to meet colleagues in the north, and mass pickets were broken up by the police.

3 According to the **dual state thesis**, issues concerning the consumption sector (such as welfare) are decided pluralistically, but issues concerning the production sector are decided in a corporatist way which favours business interests.

Study point

On a sheet of A4 complete a table:

THEORIES OF THE STATE	KEY IDEA	TWO POINTS OF CRITICISM

MORE POINTS OF EVALUATION

1 Elitist theories of power see conspiracy everywhere: the 'three Cs' (consciousness, cohesion, conspiracy) lurk behind every major political event. But much in politics is accidental, unplanned, and the outcome of chance and a lack of intelligence rather than being the result of deliberate conspiracy.
2 Marxist theories fail to explain how power in post-revolutionary societies will be subjected to democratic control. In the *State and Revolution* (1917) **Lenin** declared that any cook could run the state – but the subsequent history of the Soviet Union showed that it was not that simple! (Perhaps Lenin means 'crook' rather than 'cook'.) **Robert McKenzie** suggested that his colleague Ralph Miliband, author of *The State in Capitalist Society*, should write a sequel called *The State in Communist Society*.
3 Pluralist theories view politics through rose-coloured spectacles. At the lower level of power there are a wide variety of groups which have a real say in policy-making. But at the upper level of power key decision-making is in the hands of the few.

TOTALITARIANISM, TERROR, AND IDEOLOGICAL CONTROL

In *Totalitarian Dictatorship and Democracy* (1956) **Friedrich and Brzezinski** list six characteristic features of totalitarian societies:

1 an official ideology which everyone is supposed to support;
2 a single mass party, usually led by one person;
3 a monopoly of control of all military weapons;

4 central control of the economy;
5 a monopoly over all means of mass communication;
6 a system of terroristic police control.

In *One Dimensional Man* **Herbert Marcuse** introduces the concept of 'non-terroristic totalitarianism'. Political leaders in the USA, unlike those of Stalinist Russia or Nazi Germany, do not use terror to stay in power. But in Marcuse's view, the USA can still be described as 'totalitarian'. This is because its population has been indoctrinated by advertising and television into accepting a single ideology – the ideology of mass culture consumerism. 'Can one really distinguish between the mass media as instruments of information and entertainment, and as agents of manipulation and indoctrination?' (1964). Friedrich and Brzezinski see terror as a key feature of totalitarianism. But for Marcuse terror is simply a means to an end: it is one of a number of ways which can be used to control the population. In societies such as the USA and the UK totalitarian control is achieved by the more subtle means of media indoctrination.

Study point

In small groups discuss:

1 whether a society which lacks a 'system of terroristic police control' can still be described as totalitarian; and
2 to what extent are schools, hospitals or prisons totalitarian institutions?

Study point

The following quotations describe totalitarian, corporate, power elitist, capitalist, new class, and pluralist definitions of the State. Which is which?

1 *... the state recognises the different interests of which society is composed by fostering their organisation in separate nation-wide institutions which both represent and control their members, and then provides a forum within which their mutually complementary needs are harmonised.'*

2 *'...through the total permeation of all institutions by the Communist party, the restrictions on membership and the advantages that accrue to membership, a kind of self-perpetuating power structure asserts itself that has all the characteristics associated with a ruling class...'*

3 *'...this elite group was composed of three loosely interlocking groups, who had come to occupy the pivotal positions of power in modern American society: the heads of industry, military leaders, and leading politicians.'*

4 *'A dictatorial form of centralised government that regulates every aspect of state and private behaviour.'*

5 *'...power is shared among a multiplicity of groups and organisations.'*

6 *'By definition, the ruling class exercises its ruling power over other classes and strata through the state – through holding state power. Consequently, two relationships must be ensured. The state, particularly its commanding personnel, must* represent *that is to say, promote and defend the ruling class and its mode of exploitation or supremacy. At the same time, the State must* mediate *the exploitation or domination of the ruling class over other classes and strata.'*

Answers on page 135.

Study point

Information on the State in the USA can be explored on the following two websites:

- The White House: http://www.whitehouse.gov/
- The CIA: http://www.odci.gov/cia/

DEMOCRACY

Democracy means 'rule by the people' or 'people power'. (The Greek *demos* means people and *kratos* means power). **Ste. Croix** refers to 'the extraordinary originality of Greek democracy, which in the fundamental sense of *taking political decisions by majority vote of all citizens*, occurred earlier than in any other society we know about' (1981). Democracy was practised in the city-state of Athens between 5 and 4 BC. All citizens were able to participate in decision-making and exercise political power. However, Athens was a slave-owning state and less than a quarter of its population had rights of citizenship. No female, or male aged under 30, or slave, could be a citizen.

THE EARLY PHILOSOPHERS

Pericles (circa 490–429 BC) believed that individuals could only fulfil themselves and develop their personalities by actively participating in civic life. In his view politics was not a specialised activity to be carried out by an elite. All citizens were capable of being 'sound judges of policy'.

Plato (circa 428–348 BC) was a critic of democracy. He believed that the 'royal science' of government should be in the hands – not of the people – but of an intellectual elite of philosopher–kings.

Plato's pupil, **Aristotle**, (384–322 BC) also had a negative view of democracy and saw it as representing the rule of the ignorant and unenlightened masses.

Activity

In small groups:

1 Outline a case in favour of Pericles' view that ordinary citizens have the ability to participate in political decision-making.
2 Outline a case in favour of Plato's view that only a minority of the population – the intellectual elite – has the ability to participate in political decision-making.

DIRECT DEMOCRACY

The system of democracy developed in ancient Athens was based on direct democracy.

- The sovereign law-making body was the *General Assembly of Citizens* which met some 40 times each year. As many as 6,000 citizens may have participated in its debates.
- A smaller executive body, the *Council*, was responsible for putting the Assembly's decisions into effect and carrying out administration. This was composed of some 500 members who were elected by lot each year.

The French political philosopher **Jean-Jacques Rousseau** believed that only direct democracy could ensure individual liberty. His *Social Contract* (1762) declares that 'The English people think that they are free; but in this belief they are wrong. They are free only when they are electing members of Parliament. Once the election has been completed, they revert to a condition of slavery: they are nothing'.

Elected representatives represent no one but themselves. In the UK democracy is based on **indirect** or **representative democracy**. Citizenship alone (unlike the case in ancient Athens) does not entitle individuals to walk into the legislature and participate in debates and law-making. Instead Members of Parliament pass laws on the public's behalf.

MPs use their own judgement of what is in the public interest. They are not delegates to be instructed or mandated to support or oppose particular policies by those who voted for them. In a speech to his Bristol constituents in 1774 **Edmund Burke** declared: 'Your representative owes you not his industry only but his judgements; and he betrays, instead of serving you, if he sacrifices it to your opinion.'

Activity

In small groups:

1 Examine ways in which new forms of direct democracy could be developed.
2 Suggest an issue of some concern to your school, college or local neighbourhood. Consider the possible value of direct democracy in achieving a solution.
3 Examine the argument that in complex societies with large populations the only practical form of democracy is indirect or representative democracy.

LEADING THEORISTS

Barbara Goodwin describes the central tenets of democracy as:

1 Supremacy of the people.
2 The consent of the governed as the basis of legitimacy.
3 The rule of law – peaceful methods of conflict resolution.
4 The existence of a common good or public interest.
5 The value of the individual as a rational, moral, active citizen.
6 Equal civil rights for all individuals (1997).

Barrington Moore, Jr. sees the development of democracy as involving 'a long and certainly incomplete struggle to do three closely related things':

1 to check arbitrary rulers;
2 to replace arbitrary rules with just and rational ones; and
3 to obtain a share for the underlying population in the making of rules (1966).

David Beetham writes that the idea of democracy

> 'can be expressed in the twin principles of popular control and popular sovereignty. The rules and policies of any group, association or people should be subject to control by its members, so that they reflect their choices and preferences; the members should have equal influence and equal consideration in the framing of these rules and policies.'
>
> ('Bite the Ballot' supplement to the *New Statesman*, 29.4.94).

DEMOCRACY IN THE UK

The extension of the franchise was a key factor in the establishment of democracy in the UK.

- The right to vote was extended to the male middle class by the First Reform Act of 1832. This still left 95 per cent of the adult population unenfranchised.
- The Second Reform Act of 1867 extended the right to vote to skilled male manual workers. This left 87 per cent of the adult population unenfranchised.
- Women did not obtain the right to vote on the same terms as men until 1928.
- In 1969 the voting age was lowered from 21 to 18.
- In 1989 people who had lived abroad for up to 20 years were granted the right to vote.
- Some groups of the population, such as persons of unsound mind, peers, felons (those in prison for a year or more) and the Monarch, do not have the right to vote).

Non-democratic features of the UK political system

In the UK political system the following non-democratic features continue to exist:

- The head of state, the Monarch, is not elected.
- The unelected House of Lords can revise legislation and delay for a year laws passed by the House of Commons.
- **Leys** notes that there are no elections for judges and magistrates as there are in the USA, 'nor is there any popular "initiative" as there is in Switzerland. No popular voice is heard in the selection of the board of any nationalised industry, the board of governors of the BBC or the Independent Television Authority...' (1986).

Extension of democracy in the UK

Proposals to extend democracy in the UK include:

1. More frequent use of local and national referendums.
2. Replacing the existing 'first-past-the-post' electoral system with proportional representation.
3. Giving employees more of a say in decision-making at their place of work.
4. Setting up citizens' juries (whereby members of the public investigate specific

issues in depth and then pass their findings on to elected representatives).

5 Establishing new regional and national parliaments with effective law-making and tax-raising powers.
6 Electing members of the House of Lords.
7 Changing the culture of political organisations so that meetings become more open and inclusive.
8 Revitalising local government by increasing the powers of councils; introducing direct elections of mayors; switching election days from Thursdays to weekends; allowing voting to take place at new venues (such as supermarkets); increasing voter turn-out at local elections by making it easier to register on the electoral roll.

POINTS OF EVALUATION

1 In modern societies practical problems make it difficult to apply the pure form of direct democracy developed in ancient Athens.
2 Indirect or representative democracy has been criticised because representatives follow party lines rather than consulting the electors or acting according to their own conscience (eg Peter Temple-Morris was elected with a large majority as a Conservative MP in 1997 but became a Labour MP in 1998 because he opposed the policy of the leadership – after crossing the floor of the House he did not stand for re-election in his constituency).
3 In the USA there are far more elective positions (eg judges) than in the UK. The head of State (the President) is elected, whereas in the UK the position of head of State is an inherited one.
4 There is continuing ideological debate over whether better ways can be found of organising the political system than indirect representative democracy.

SUMMARY

- According to Max Weber the defining feature of the State is its monopoly of the legitimate use of force.
- States seek to exercise *de facto* sovereignty power as well as *de jure* authority over a specific territory.
- Totalitarian States are one-party dictatorships which seek to control the ideas and beliefs of their citizens.
- The State in western societies has been analysed in terms of the power elite State, the neo-corporate State, the capitalist State, and the pluralist State.
- The concept of democracy or people power was first formulated in ancient Athens.
- The two main forms of democracy are direct democracy and indirect or representative democracy.
- Male members of the British working class were first granted the right to vote in 1867.
- Until 1928 adult women aged under 30 years were denied the right to vote.

Group work

Divide into small groups. Each group formulates a proposal aimed at increasing democratic participation in the UK. This is followed by a discussion on which of the proposals put forward is likely to be the most practical and effective.

Key Concepts activity

1 In your own words explain the following terms: *de facto* sovereignty; totalitarianism; the Iron Law of Oligarchy; direct and indirect democracy.

2 In small groups discuss the validity of the following two quotations:
- 'The state is nothing but a machine for the oppression of one class by another…' (F. Engels).
- 'The dictatorship of the official and not of the worker is on the march.' (M. Weber).

Practice questions

1 '…We have all become democrats in theory at just the stage in history at which it has become virtually impossible for us in practice to organise our social life in a democratic fashion any longer.' (From John Dunn, *Western Political Theory In The Face Of The Future* (1993). Explain and discuss.

2 Compare and contrast the concepts of the pluralist and the totalitarian state.

Coursework

1 Investigate levels of voter turn-out in recent local government elections, general elections and elections to the European Parliament held in the area in which you live. What do turn-out levels tell us about the vitality of representative democracy in the UK?

2 Interview members of the local political elite (eg councillors, MPs, MEPs, party activists) and find out their views on the effectiveness of democracy in the UK. What measures (if any) do they feel could be introduced to increase democracy participation and accountability?

4

IDEOLOGIES

Introduction

THIS CHAPTER EXAMINES the concept of ideology which was first formulated some two centuries ago. An ideology serves as a guide to behaviour. It consists of a set of ideas about society and politics which is both descriptive and prescriptive. While Marxist theorists see ideology as guiding behaviour in ways which advance the interests of the dominant class, functionalist theorists focus on the role of shared beliefs in integrating society together and increasing social cohesion. Leading political ideologies of the twentieth century include conservatism, liberalism, socialism, communism, nationalism, and fascism. A number of new ideologies have come to the fore in recent decades. In the 1950s and 1960s theorists spoke of an 'end of ideology' and in the 1990s of the 'end of history'. Since the French Revolution of 1789 ideologies have been classified as being on the Left or the Right. 'Third Way' theorists claim that it is possible to 'go beyond' the division between Left and Right.

DEFINING IDEOLOGY

The term 'ideology' was coined in 1795 by the French philosopher **Antoine Destutt de Tracy**. He defined it as the scientific study of ideas. The term is used today to refer to clusters or sets of ideas about society and politics which guide behaviour and have a practical impact on the world. Ideology is a form of *applied philosophy* which can change power relationships in society. Ideologies are action-directing beliefs which describe how things are and prescribe how things should be. They are forms of discourse (meaning expressed in language) which can have a powerful impact on politics and history.

Table 3: *Theorists, concepts and issues in this chapter*		
KEY THEORISTS	KEY CONCEPTS	KEY ISSUES
de Tracy (1754–1863)	Ideology	• Study of ideas
Durkheim (1858–1917)	Collective beliefs	• Integrate society together
Weber (1864–1920)	Elective affinity	• Social groups are predisposed to support particular types of ideology
Marx (1818–83), Engels (1820–95)	Class and ideology	• Ideology distorts the truth and advances class interests
Burke (1729–97)	Conservatism	• Stability and gradual change
Mill (1806–73)	Liberalism	• Liberty and the self-governing citizen
Webb (1859–1947)	Socialism	• Public ownership, planning, and control of the commanding heights of the economy
Marx	Communism	• Revolutionary change and the establishment of a classless society based on common ownership
Hobsbawm (b. 1917)	Nationalism	• The invention of national identity
Mussolini (1883–1945)	Fascism	• Ultra-nationalism and the establishment of a one-party State
Lovelock (b. 1919)	Green ecology	• Gaia – viewing the earth as a living entity
French revolutionaries	Left and Right	• Classification of ideologies along a single axis

- Weber noted that '...very frequently the "world images" which have been created by "ideas" have, like switchmen, determined the tracks along which action has been pushed by the dynamic of interests'.
- **Jorge Luis Borges**, an Argentian novelist, described how ideology can seize hold of the imagination and transform political reality. In the 1940s 'any symmetry with a semblance of order – dialectical materialism, anti-Semitism, Nazism – was sufficient to entrance the minds of men' (1970).
- **Terry Eagleton** refers to 'a poem by Thom Gunn of a German conscript in the Second World War who risked his life helping Jews escape the fate in store for them at the hands of the Nazis:

"I know he had unusual eyes.
Whose power no orders could determine.
Not to mistake the men he saw,
As others did, for gods or vermin."'

Eagleton adds: 'What persuades men and women to mistake each other from time to time for gods or vermin is ideology' (1991).

- Science – unlike ideology – is primarily concerned with empirical investigation and the pursuit of truth. 'A scientific hypothesis is one that could always in principle be falsified; whereas it is hard to see how one could falsify a cry like "Reclaim the Night!", or "Long live the Fatherland!"'.

Study point

What ideology do you subscribe to? Note down some of your key ideological beliefs. To what extent are these related to your membership of particular social groups?

POINTS OF EVALUATION

1. All thinking can be seen as 'ideological' in the broad sense that it involves a specific world-view of how society 'ticks'. Everyone has an *ideology mark 1* – a distinctive way of looking at society.
2. Some individuals have an *ideology mark 2* – a clearly articulated and coherent set of political ideas and beliefs.
3. The term ideology is sometimes used in the pejorative sense of a set of beliefs which are closed, fixed and rigid. *Ideology mark 3* refers to dogmatic sets of political ideas which are not susceptible to reasoned debate and evidence. (Eagleton notes that 'nobody would claim that their own thinking was ideological, just as nobody would habitually refer to themself as Fatso. Ideology, like halitosis, is in this sense what the other person has'.)

THE 'FALSITY–TRUTH' CONTINUUM OF IDEOLOGIES

All ideologies involve sets of ideas which simplify a complex social and political reality. But some ideologies are more simplistic and less truthful than others.

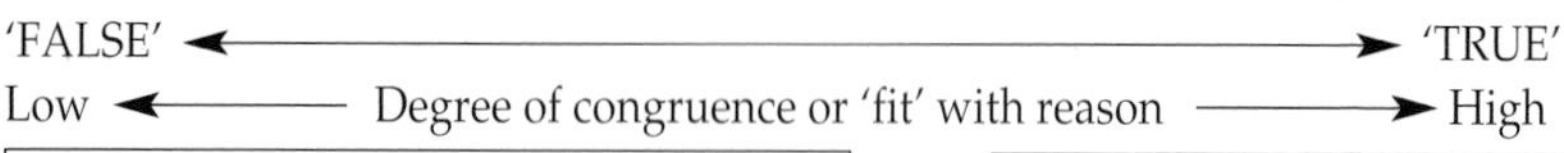

eg 'Only human beings with red hair who were sent to earth by Zog of Planet Pluto should have the right to live.'

eg 'All human beings should have the right to live.'

THE 'FALSITY–TRUTH' CONTINUUM OF IDEOLOGIES

THEORISTS AND DEBATES

Functionalist theorists refer to **value-consensus** rather than ideology. The dominant beliefs are seen as furthering the interests of society at large rather than (as conflict theorists believe) the interests of the powerful.

Émile Durkheim saw core beliefs and values as the cultural 'cement' which holds society together. In order to achieve social order and stability individuals are socialised into accepting key institutions and beliefs. Rituals, ceremonies, and special symbols (such as the national flag and anthem) serve to reinforce emotional identification with society. Symbolic structures form 'ideological communities' which bind individuals to their society. For Durkheim the central sources of social integration are 'rules, custom, habit, prejudices and sympathy as opposed to reason and interests…' (Lukes, 1973).

Max Weber believed there is an **elective affinity** between particular types of ideology and particular social strata. Social groups are 'idea-prone': individuals subscribe to beliefs which their life circumstances give them an emotional sympathy with. Low status groups have an elective affinity with evangelical-style religions. High status groups have an elective affinity with conservative ideologies.

Karl Marx analysed ideologies in terms of sets of ideas which distort and obscure the truth and shape behaviour in ways which advance the political and economic interests of the dominant class. Members of the working class who support the dominant bourgeois ideology are victims of what **Friedrich Engels**, Marx's intellectual collaborator, called **false consciousness**. That is they believe in ideas which – in the marxist view – are not only untrue but which serve to promote the interests of those who exploit them.)

Antonio Gramsci, an Italian neo-marxist, formulated the concept of hegemony or cultural leadership (from the Greek word *hegemon* meaning ruler or chieftain). A hegemonic class wins consent for its rule from members of other social classes. A process of ideological incorporation ensures that large sections of the population come to view the hegemonic ideas as 'common sense'. According to the **dominant ideology thesis** the survival of capitalist society can be explained in terms of hegemony. The working class has been persuaded to accept the mode of thinking of the ruling class. Ideas – not coercion and the threat of State violence – constitute the key to social stability. **Georg Lukács**, a Hungarian neo-marxist, believed that the social location of the working class enables it to 'see through' the myths and illusions of the dominant ideology. In *History and Class Consciousness* (1922) he argued that, by actively participating in political struggle, workers become the subject rather than the object of history and thereby take control of their lives. Workers' position in the class system makes it possible for them to understand the interlocking structures – the 'social totality' – of their society.

Karl Mannheim distinguished between ideologies – sets of ideas which defend existing interests and attempt to keep things as they are – and **utopias** – sets of ideas which seek to bring about social change. In *Ideology and Utopia* (1919) he rejected the view that the working class occupies some kind of epistemologically privileged position (ie has superior knowledge and insight) which enables it to see through ideology and grasp the real 'truth' about society. The experience of members of *all* classes is partial and limited. *Every* social class is predisposed to support ideologies which further its own sectional interests. Only intellectuals – free-floating and declassed seekers of truth and reason – are able to resist the distortions of ideology.

Seymore Martin Lipset and **Daniel Bell** formulated the **end of ideology thesis**. This was first put forward some 40 years ago and claims that the major social problems facing western industrial societies have been solved, the 'isms' and ideologies of the past (such as communism, socialism, fascism etc) no longer have any relevance, and a new era of consensus politics based on de-seated agreement between the major political parties has arrived. Echoes of the end of ideology thesis can be heard in the **end of history thesis** of **Francis Fukuyama** (1992). He declared that the 'liberal *idea*' is emerging victorious: 'for a very large part of the world, there is now no ideology with pretentions to universality that is in a position to challenge liberal democracy…'.

J. S. McClelland refers to **non-communicating discourse groups**. These are groups which seek to impose their ideology on the rest of society and exclude and eliminate all other points of view. For pluralists 'not getting everything you want, and appearing to be a good loser, is part of the game'. But some groups refuse to play by pluralist rules and are convinced that their ideology – and only their ideology – represents the truth (1996).

Study point

Consider and explain which of the following views might be attributed to Weber, Marx, or Durkheim.

1. the majority of the population have a dominant ideology imposed on them. They are victims of 'false consciousness' (a kind of delusion which is mistakenly thought to be true). Some groups fail to see how they are exploited and accept their lot.
2. Social cohesion demands that members of society share common values. These are vital if order and stability are to be maintained. Shared beliefs are a functional necessity – not a matter of ideological delusion. Societies best fulfill the needs of their members when there is common acceptance of core cultural symbols and institutions.
3. Ideas can shape social life, but they are not necessarily the products of class interests. People will always endeavour to justify their social position by moral arguments about their rights to exercise control. The commands of the holders of power will be accepted as legitimate if they are exercised in a lawful and consensual way.

POINTS OF EVALUATION

1 There are similarities between functionalist and Marxist analysis. Both see ideology as being composed of concepts, ideas, myths, and images which shape the ways in which people behave in their everyday lives. But functionalists focus on the positive functions of ideology while Marxists focus on the negative functions of ideology.
2 In Gramsci's view the ideological hegemony exerted by the dominant class has to be decisively broken if revolutionary change is to take place. Yet as the dominant class controls the means of communication (a key source of hegemony) it is difficult to see just how this will happen. 'How is the working class to take power in a social formation where the dominant power is subtly, pervasively diffused throughout habitual daily practices, intimately interwoven with "culture" itself, inscribed in the very texture of our experience from nursery school to funeral parlour?' (Eagleton).
3 Critics of the dominant ideology thesis argue that it is not hegemony but what Marx called 'the dull compulsion of the economic' – the routine pressures of economic survival – which explains the survival of the existing social order. The mass of the population remains deeply divided over ideological issues, and it is only within the dominant class that there a high degree of ideological agreement. **Abercrombie** et al see the dominant ideology as having little influence on the rest of the population (1980). (Yet ideology must play *some* part in maintaining the social order).
4 **John Plamenatz** criticises Lukács for assuming 'that, however much the workers' conditions improve under capitalism, they will never improve so much that the workers acquire interests and an ideology in keeping with the established order' (1970). The same criticism can be directed against other Marxist theorists such as Gramsci.
5 **Alvin Gouldner** rejects Mannheim's view that intellectuals are exempt from ideological bias. Intellectuals are not free-floating or declassed individuals. They are members of a self-seeking group – a 'new class' – which has sectional interests of its own.
6 Critics of the end of ideology thesis see it as an ideology in its own right – an ideology which celebrated the status quo of 1950s and 60s America. Francis Fukuyama's thesis that liberal democracy was the new and undefeated Heavyweight Champion of World Ideology received a boost from the collapse of Soviet and Eastern European communism in 1989. But other ideological challengers will be sure to step into the ring: the 'end of history' is still some way off.
7 Metanarratives seek to explain the Meaning of History. But in the pomo or postmodern view such explanations are built on sand: there is no meaning to history other than that which individuals choose to give it. In today's media-saturated world moral absolutes have been undermined and group identities

weakened. The rock solid foundations of ideological, scientific and religious certainties have crumbled and a proliferation of consumer lifestyles now grow over their ruins.

THE LEFT-WING—RIGHT-WING CLASSIFICATION

In 1789 the French King Louis XVI called a meeting of the Estates General. This consisted of clergy (the First Estate), aristocracy (the Second Estate), and commoners (the Third Estate). The aristocracy sat on the King's right and the commoners sat on the King's left. This is the historical origin of the terms 'leftwing' and 'rightwing'. The left favours equality and the redistribution of wealth and power. The Right regards inequality as inevitable and favours the preservation of individual property rights and the limitation of State power. The Left sides with 'labour'. The right claims that by safeguarding the interests of 'capital' they are safeguarding the interests of society at large.

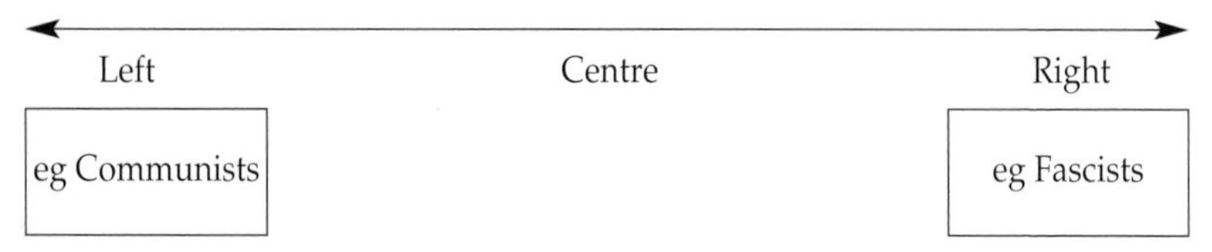

THE POLITICAL SPECTRUM FROM LEFT TO RIGHT WING

Critics of the leftwing–rightwing classification argue that:

1 It ignores the distinction between 'tough and authoritarian' politics and 'tender and democratic' politics. On this axis the extreme Left and the extreme Right belong to the *same* end of the political spectrum: both have supported dictatorial policies and have been intolerant of dissent.

AN ALTERNATIVE POLITICAL SPECTRUM

(Note) survey research in the UK has found that 20 per cent of the population are 'authoritarian' (they favour firm government control on both economic and moral matters) – and 20 per cent are 'libertarian' (they are opposed to government control).

2 On many key political questions (such as the development of the European Union, the UK's policy on a Single European Currency, global warming, and animal rights) there is no obvious leftwing or rightwing 'position'.
3 The rise of 'postmaterialist' politics has made quality of life issues central to political debate. It is difficult to analyse such issues as the environment, town planning, the pursuit of economic growth, and preferred forms of family life in traditional leftwing–rightwing terms.

INEQUALITY, LEFT AND RIGHT

In 1996 – according to the *UN Development Report* – the total wealth of the world's top 358 billionaires was equal to the combined incomes of 2.3 billion people (45 per cent of the world's population). For the Left the social problems caused by such inequality can only be tackled by introducing radical policies of wealth redistribution. For the Right it is only by encouraging the entrepreneurial skills of the 358 billionaires and increasing economic growth that opportunities will be created for people to escape from poverty.

Activity

In small groups discuss whether the terms 'left-wing' and 'right-wing' continue to be relevant today.

THE THIRD WAY

Theorists and political leaders speak of a 'Third Way' in politics which is neither on the Left or on the Right. Both the First Way – capitalism – and the Second Way – socialism – are said to have failed. In President Clinton's view, 'We have moved past the sterile debate between those who say government is the enemy and those who say government is the answer. My fellow Americans, we have found a Third Way.' According to Giddens, the Third Way is an attempt at adapting social democracy 'to a world which has changed fundamentally over the past two or three decades'. Its aim is 'to help citizens pilot their way through the major revolutions of our time: globalisation, transformations in personal life and our relationship to nature'. 'No rights without responsibilities' could be 'the prime motto for the new politics' (Giddens, 1998).

Third Way politics aim at breaking out of the conventional leftwing–rightwing straightjacket and winning the support of the 'radical centre'. It follows the Left in valuing social solidarity and promoting opportunities for the socially excluded. It follows the Right in valuing private enterprise and encouraging individual responsibility. According to Tony Blair 'it is a third way because it moves decisively beyond an Old Left preoccupied by state control, high taxation and producer interests; and a New Right treating public investment, and often the very notions of "society" and collective endeavour, as evils to be undone'. Critics of the Third Way such as J. K. Galbraith describe it as a political response to changes in the class structure: 'The increase in numbers and power of the middle-income groups means that governments choose to meet their needs first. The Third Way is a justification of that necessity.' Other critics see the concept of the Third Way as lacking theoretical coherence. It is a 'Two and a Quarter Way', an uneasy mixture of First Way ideas (support for a market-driven, capitalist economy and the structural inequalities which go with it), Second Way ideas (State intervention to ameliorate and reduce social disadvantage), topped up with communitarian moralism.

Activity

In small groups discuss whether there can be a 'Third Way' in politics which is neither on the Left or on the Right. Can governments introduce policies which both encourage private enterprise and economic competitiveness *and* reduce poverty and social exclusion?

POLITICAL IDEOLOGIES

CONSERVATISM

Conservatism seeks to preserve what is best in the existing framework of society. The Conservative Party can be traced back to the Royalist or Court group of the seventeenth century. The Court group was known as the 'Tories' – 'Tory' being an Irish outlaw. (Defenders of the status quo used Irish soldiers to support the Stuart Monarch.) In his 1834 election address to the constituents of Tamworth, Sir Robert Peel declared that his Party sought to 'conserve' all that was good in existing institutions. Tories were subsequently known as Conservatives. Disraeli's extension of the vote to the male working class in 1867 led the Party to transform itself from an elite faction into a mass party with locally based organisation in constituencies.

Key themes of conservative ideology focus on: the value of stability and the benefits of preserving established institutions; the dangers of radical change; the need for hierarchy and inequality.

Views of Conservatism

- Edmund Burke was a Whig rather than a Tory MP. But he has had a major influence on conservative ideology. Burke celebrated the value of tradition and continuity and warned against the costs of embarking on programmes of radical change. He believed these would destroy the priceless legacy handed down by past generations.
- **Benjamin Disraeli** (the first Earl of Beaconsfield and Prime Minister, February–December 1868 and 1874–80) declared that the 'first object' of the Conservative Party was 'to maintain the institutions of the country'. He warned against the political dangers of a class-divided 'two nations' society and advocated 'Tory democracy' as a way of integrating the working class into the established order.
- For **Michael Oakeshott** conservatism is a 'disposition'. 'To be conservative is to prefer the known to the unknown, to prefer the tried to the untried, fact to mystery, the actual to the possible, the limited to the unbounded…'.
- Anthony Giddens writes that 'if conservatism means anything' it means 'the desire to conserve – and specifically the conserving of tradition, as the "inherited wisdom of the past"' (1994). Conservatives have a pessimistic view of human nature and believe that projects of radical political change are doomed to end in failure.
- William Waldegrave (who was a minister in Margaret Thatcher's radical Conservative Government) wrote that 'a devillish Fu Manchu, engaged in a plan to leave Britain feeling angry, bewildered, and fragmented, could do worse than to start by abolishing familiar weights and measures, currency, policeman's uniforms, postage stamp designs, letter box colours, radio and television programmes, brand names, modes of address… there ought to be a severe limitation on the speed of change with regard to those laws, regulations, and customs which directly affect how people live – if we value the stability of communities (1978).

An anti-ideological ideology

Conservatives distrust the concept of ideology and conservatism itself has been described as an anti-ideological ideology. **David Willetts** notes that 'Conservatives are wary of grand statements of principles and beliefs. Many attribute the political success of British conservatism to its pragmatism – its concern with political practice not political theory. Anything that goes further than this is dismissed as ideology…'. He points out that 'Conservatives have not aimed, like some reactionary continental movements, to halt all change. Indeed, it is because the conservative recognises that change is both inevitable and costly that there is often a note of melancholy in British conservative thought…' (1992).

Conservatism and the social hierarchy

Defence of the social hierarchy – the division of society into different ranks of status – is a central tenet of conservatism. 'Running through all the varieties of conservatism is the theme of inequality. Conservatives stress the benefits to society of a ruling class whereby a rich and powerful minority guide and restrain the conduct of a majority.' But this approval of social hierarchy is usually blended 'with the entrepreneurial message of self-help' (**Eccleshall**, 1984).

Birch (1998) summarises traditional conservatism in six points:

1 a sceptical view of human nature
2 society as an organic unity which is bound together by feelings of mutual obligation
3 inequality as an inescapable fact of life
4 following the writings of Burke, individual human reason is not adequate to the task of formulating a theory of good government from scratch
5 opposition to radical changes in institutions and policies
6 the proper role of government is to protect the weaker members of society from exploitation.

Thatcherism

During the period of Margaret Thatcher's leadership of the Conservative Party (1975–90) the doctrine of entrepreneurial individualism (a central ideological theme of liberalism) was in the ascendancy. **Thatcherism** has been interpreted as:

1 *A new radical ideology of authoritarian populism*: economic policies were based on neo-liberalism (monetarism, tax cuts, privatisation, extension of market forces, etc).
2 *A return to traditional conservatism*: the emphasis on a strong State and a free economy, law and order, defence of property rights, and reduced taxation would have been supported by most past leaders of the Conservative Party.
3 *A new political style*: in practice, most Thatcherite policies were based on a pragmatic approach. What was distinctive was 'no-nonsense' leadership, a disdain for talk of compromise, and a rhetorical appeal to traditional moral values.
4 *A reflection of a changed social structure and higher material living standards*: in the view of Lord Blake: 'if the "rich" in one sense of the word have now become the majority, if the division between the two nations is much lower down the social scale than it was, that could explain the success of the "populism" which carried the Conservatives to victory...'. Thatcherism appealed to the aspirations of the new affluent majority of the population.

Study point

In small groups discuss whether 'Thatcherism' was a continuation of Conservatism, or a radical break with Conservatism.

LIBERALISM

Liberalism is defined by *The Oxford Dictionary of Politics* (1996) as 'the belief that it is the aim of politics to preserve individual rights and to maximise freedom of choice'. Liberals have an optimistic belief in the rationality of human beings and their capacity for progress and social improvement.

Prior to 1830, the Liberals were known as Whigs (the Whiggamores being Scottish Presbyterian rebels opposed to the Stuart monarchy). While support for the Conservatives was drawn from the protectionist landed gentry, support for the free-trading Liberals came from new commercial and manufacturing interests.

Between 1867 and 1918 the Liberal Party alternated with the Conservative Party as the main Party of government. **William Gladstone** was one of the founders of modern liberalism. He was Prime Minister from 1868–74; 1880–5; February–August of 1886; and 1892–4. The last Liberal Prime Minister was **Lloyd George** who headed a coalition Government from 1916–22. A revival of support for the Liberal Party took place in the early 1960s. From 1981–7 the Liberal Party formed an alliance with the Social Democratic Party and became the Liberal Democrats in 1989.

The foundations of the modern Welfare State (unemployment and sickness benefits, and pensions) were constructed by the Liberal Governments of 1905–16. In 1942 William Beveridge (a Liberal) published his *Report on Social Insurance and Allied Services* which sought to defeat the 'five giants' of want, idleness, ignorance, squalor, and disease.

Liberalism and liberty

John Stuart Mill distinguished between *self-regarding actions* (which only effect the individual concerned) and *other-regarding actions* (which effect other people). (Critics claim that *every* action taken by an individual effects other people.) Liberty will be threatened if individuals' self-regarding actions are subjected to State regulation and control. In *Utilitarianism* (1841) Mill wrote that 'The only purpose for which power can be rightfully exercised over any member of a civilised community, against his own will, is to prevent harm to others'.

Liberalism emphasises the value of contract and consent. Constitutionalism and law are seen as key safeguards of human liberty: 'If proper procedures for making and executing laws can be devised and enforced constitutionally, the risk of arbitrary or tyrannical rule is minimised.' Social justice should be based on merit so that individuals 'gain rewards in proportion to their talents and merits and in exchange for their contribution to society…'. Tolerance is highly valued and liberalism 'passed unfavourable judgements on societies which suppress dissidence and nonconformist views' (Goodwin, 1997).

Classic liberalism supported *laissez-faire* ('leave alone') economic policies of free trade, a minimal state, and individual self-reliance. However, the **New Liberalism**

of the late nineteenth century supported the concept of the interventionist state. A key theorist was T. H. Green who believed that the State could create conditions which enable individuals to pursue moral self-improvement.

The focus of classic liberalism was on **negative liberty**: individuals should be free to pursue their own goals without interference. The focus of the New Liberalism was on **positive liberty**: individuals who are ill, uneducated, and trapped in poverty must be helped by the state if they are to be free. **Libertarianism** rejects the idea of positive liberty and sees the redistributive State as a threat to individual freedom: 'We may not remove an eye from a sighted person to give to a blind one, nor redistribute friends from the popular to the lonely' (**Matthew Festenstein**, 1998). The American theorist **Robert Nozick** supports the concept of a minimal State and argues that individuals have a natural right to pursue their own goals without being subjected to political interference.

Public Choice theory (developed by **James Buchannan** and **Gordon Tullock** of Virginia Polytechnic University) also opposes policies of State intervention. Politicians and civil servants may claim to be acting in the public interest but in reality they pursue their own self-interest at the taxpayer's expense.

Neo-liberalism seeks to promote the role of market forces and individual choice, and rejects collective provision of welfare and trade union power. **F. A. von Hayek** believed that welfare state and socialist collectivism would lead to totalitarianism and a loss of individual freedom.

According to Robert Eccleshall there is one theme of agreement which runs through all the different varieties of liberalism: 'a picture of a *one-class society of self-governing citizens*.'

In summary, the key themes of liberal ideology are: the value of the individual; of liberty; and bringing about social improvement through enlightened political action.

SOCIALISM

The word 'socialism' was first used in English in 1827. The Labour Representation Committee was created in 1900 and renamed the Labour Party in 1906. While most left parties on the continent are called 'socialist' parties the name 'Labour' reflects the British Party's origins in the trade union movement. In his study, *British Political Parties* (1963), **McKenzie** notes that in its earliest days the parliamentary Labour Party 'was committed neither to the conception of the class struggle nor to any coherent socialist philosophy or programme'. But delegates from three socialist organisations – the Social Democratic Federation, the Fabian Society, and the Independent Labour Party – took part in the Party's founding conference and from time to time socialist ideas have had an influence on Labour Party policy.

In *In Place of Fear* (1952) **Aneurin Bevan** referred to public ownership as an 'all-important step' towards socialism. In a socialist society the 'commanding heights' of the economy will be subjected to democratic control.

In April 1995 the Labour Party voted to repeal Clause IV of the Party Constitution which advocated 'the common ownership of the means of production, distribution and exchange'. Clause IV was drafted by **Sidney Webb**, a Fabian socialist who believed in the 'inevitability of gradualism' (that is the culmative impact of piecemeal reform will eventually lead to the replacement of capitalism with socialism).

According to **David Coates** a socialist society 'will exist only when an entire working-class actively run their own industries and communities on democratic lines ... Such a society will undoubtedly require new institutions, including the social ownership of the entire means of production, underpinned by an effective system of participatory democracy at factory and community level' (1980). This conception of socialism is rejected by Tony Blair. He draws a sharp distinction between socialist *goals* (such as social justice) and the *means* of achieving them. 'Wholesale nationalisation' is dismissed as quite irrelevant to socialism (or 'social-ism' as he prefers to call it).

Descriptions of socialism

Leach points out that socialism 'involved a reaction against, and a radical alternative to, industrial capitalism. If political ideologies can be linked with class interests, socialism can be seen as the political ideology of the new urban working class, effectively created by industrialisation, just as conservatism was, initially, the ideology of the bourgeoisie, or manufacturing interest ... Socialists sought a radical overhaul of existing property relations, involving the transfer of the private ownership of the means of production to social ownership, and a massive redistribution of income and wealth in favour of the working classes' (1991).

Durkheim defined socialism as a 'cry of pain'. Eagleton describes a socialist as 'just someone who is unable to get over his or her astonishment that most people who have lived and died have spent lives of wretched, fruitless, unremitting toil'.

Forms of socialism

Some forms of socialism have emphasised centralised planning, State intervention, and control from the centre. Others have emphasised decentralisation, local autonomy, and workers' self-management. It is more accurate to speak of social*isms* than social*ism*. *Revolutionary* socialism envisages a total and dramatic break with the structure and culture of existing society. *Reformist* socialism envisages an evolutionary process of piecemeal gradualism and incremental change. *Pluralist* socialism rejects the view that only the working class can be an effective agency of progressive change, and affirms the importance of civil society in which a variety of groups and associations can flourish. *Ecosocialism* attempts to blend socialist and ecological critiques of capitalism. *Market* socialism aims at combining new forms of public ownership and planning with a market economy. *Radical pragmatism* grounds proposals for socialist change in the here and now rather than devising blueprints for a utopian future (**Tony Fitzpatrick**, 1998).

In summary, key themes of socialist ideology are: public ownership; greater equality; advancing the interests of the working class; extending democratic participation.

Activity

It was reported in July 1997 that Baroness Thatcher was seeking to establish a Professorship of Economic Free Enterprise at Cambridge University. Her foundation would provide £1.9 million to set it up. A *Guardian* editorial declared: 'Beware ideologues, even bearing gifts.'

In small groups discuss the following questions:

1 Should university professorships be established with ideological titles such as 'Economic Free Enterprise'?
2 If you were a university administrator, and a leftwing businessman or woman offered a similar amount to set up a Professorship of Socialist Achievement, what would be your response?
3 Should individuals with strong 'ideological' views be appointed to University Professorships?

COMMUNISM

In the *Communist Manifesto* (1848) Karl Marx and Freidrich Engels distinguish communism from other forms of socialism which were current at the time.

- *Feudal* socialism and *petty bourgeois* socialism were both seen as having a romantic and nostalgic view of the preindustrial past.
- *Conservative* socialism aimed at 'redressing social grievances in order to secure the continued existence of bourgeois society'.
- *Utopian* socialism dreamt up impractical schemes for building 'New Jerusalems' and other 'castles in the air'.
- Only communism – a movement 'against the existing social and political order of things' which would win the support of the majority of the population (ie the working-class) – could end class exploitation, radically reduce alienation, and establish a classless and fully democratic society.

Neither Marx or Engels lived to see a communist government come to power. After their deaths a fierce controversy took place amongst Marxist theorists between those who believed that capitalism was doomed and had to be overthrown by revolution, and those who believed that it could be transformed through parliamentary reform.

Before the 1914–18 war Germany was the centre of the Marxist movement. In 1912 the German Social Democratic Party gained a third of all the votes cast. One of the Party's leading theorists – **Eduard Bernstein** – argued that the party should 'dare to appear as what it actually was: a democratic Socialist Party of reform'. In his view the analysis put forward by Marx and Engels needed to be 'revised': 'Peasants do not sink; middle class does not disappear; crises do not grow ever larger; misery and serfdom do not increase.'

Bernstein was denounced by Lenin for having abandoned the revolutionary cause. In *What Is To Be Done?* (1902) Lenin called for the creation of a disciplined, centralised and professional Communist Party organisation: 'Give us an organisation of revolutionaries, and we will overturn Russia!' In 1917 Lenin did overturn Russia: the Russian Communist Party seized power and initiated a programme of sweeping change. The model of Party organisation developed by Lenin was subsequently copied by other Communist Parties, and 'Marxist-Leninism' emerged as a distinctive ideology.

In the *Future of Socialism* (1956) **Anthony Crosland** supported the 'revisionist' view that the Marxist analysis of capitalism had ceased to have any relevance. But in *Arguments for Socialism* (1979) fellow Labour MP **Tony Benn** described Marx as 'a towering socialist philosopher who brought methods of scientific analysis to a study of society...'.

Communism today

In 1989 the communist States of Russia and Eastern Europe collapsed. Today only China, Vietnam, North Korea, and Cuba are officially communist States. But Communist Parties (or their successors) continue to be influential in Russia, Poland, Lithuania, and Italy. The Communist Party of Great Britain was founded in 1920; it reached a peak membership of 42,000 in 1942, and in 1945 two communist MPs were elected. In 1990 the Communist Party published its *Manifesto of New Times* and in 1992 was transformed into the 'Democratic Left'.

In summary, the key themes of communist ideology are: support for the international class struggle; the creation of a new type of society based on common ownership of the means of production.

NATIONALISM

During the last two centuries nationalism has had a dramatic impact on politics. 1776 (the year of the American Declaration of Independence and the first partition of Poland) and 1789 (the year of the French Revolution) signal the arrival of nationalism on the world political scene. Nationalism asserts the primacy of national identity over all other claims of allegiance. Giddens describes the nation-state as a 'bordered power-container'. A nation has been described as an 'imagined community'. Even in a very small nation is is impossible for an individual to personally know most people of the same nationality. **Benedict Anderson** argues that the development of 'print-capitalism' from the sixteenth century on 'gave a new fixity to language' and this played a crucial role in building 'the subjective idea of the nation'.

Views on nationalism

- **Modernists**, such as **Eric Hobsbawm**, see nations as 'invented traditions'. National consciousness is something which is actively created and constructed (by the creation of national languages and systems of schooling, the organisation of public ceremonies, and the building of public monuments).
- **Perennialists** reject the view that nations have been 'invented'. They believe that nations can be traced back to ethnic groups which existed in the distant past.
- **Civic Nationalism** views citizenship and allegiance to the State as the key component of national identity.
- **Ethnic nationalism** views shared ethnic characteristics as the key component of national identity. Point four of the National Socialist German Workers Party programme (NSDAP or Nazi Party) is an example of an ethnic definition of nationalism. It declared that: 'None but members of the nation may be citizens of the State. None but those of German blood, whatever their creed, may be members of the nation. No Jew, therefore, may be a member of the nation.'

Nationalism in the UK

Nationalist parties in contemporary Britain subscribe to a civic definition of nationalism. The Scottish Nationalist Party was founded in 1934, but its roots go back to 1891 when the Scottish Home Rule Association was founded. Its first MP was elected in 1945, but it was only from the mid 1960s that the SNP began to win significant support. Plaid Cymru – the Party of Wales – was founded in 1925. Its first MP was elected in 1966. Almost a fifth of the Welsh population speak Welsh, and (unlike the case in Scotland) issues of language and culture have been a key source of nationalist support. In Northern Ireland religion has served as an ethnic marker of political allegiance. Sinn Fein – 'Ourselves Alone' – (founded in 1902) has subscribed to Irish Republican nationalism and has been supported by sections of the Catholic community. Unionist Parties have represented Protestant or 'loyalist' nationalism, and (unlike Sinn Fein) have favoured the 1922 partition of Ireland into two separate States.

In summary, the key themes of nationalist ideology are: support for the principle of national self-determination and loyalty to the nation-state.

Activity

'All nations have the right to self-determination. All nations should possess their own systems of taxation, their own means of military defence, and their own states. Both Wales and Scotland are nations.'

In small groups discuss whether Wales and Scotland should become independent self-governing states.

FASCISM

The word originates from the *fasces*, the bundle of rods with a projecting axe which were the symbol of authority in ancient Rome. The first successful fascist movement was led by **Mussolini** in Italy. It was formed in 1919 and took power in 1922. Other interwar fascist movements included the Falange in Spain, the Iron Guard in Rumania, and Nazism in Germany. 'All were strongly nationalist, violently anti-Communist and anti-Marxist; all hated liberalism, democracy, and parliamentary parties, which they sought to replace by a new authoritarian state in which there could be only one party, their own, with a monopoly of power … all shared a cult of violence and action … once in power they used the power of the State to liquidate their rivals without regard for law' from *The Fontana Dictionary of Modern Thought* (1977).

A key element of Nazi ideology in Germany was racism: for Hitler the 'one enemy' was the 'Jewish Marxist Stock Exchange Press' (for anti-semites, Jewish people are either millionaires or communists). Ultra-nationalism and a yearning for a rebirth (or palingenesis) of nationalistic fervour is a hallmark of fascism.

In the view of **Kitchen** (1976) fascism:

1. is 'a phenomenon of developed industrial states'
2. was 'triggered off by a severe socio-economic crisis…'
3. was 'a response to a large and well organised working class…'
4. 'recruits its mass following from a politicised, threatened, and frightened petit bourgeoisie'
5. 'fascist regimes are characterised by an alliance between the fascist party leadership and the traditional elites of industry, banking, the bureaucracy and the military'
6. 'fascism is a terror regime which dispenses with all the trappings of parliamentary democracy'
7. 'fascist regimes pursue aggressive and expansionist foreign political aims'.

THE BRUTAL CRUELTY OF APARTHEID IN SOUTH AFRICA (PICTURE TAKEN IN CAPE TOWN, 1976)

H. H. Trevor-Roper points out that 'fascism properly, what I have called "dynamic fascism" – the cult of force, contemptuous of religious and traditional ideas, the self-assertion of an inflamed lower middle class in a weakened industrial society – is radically different from ideological conservatism, the traditional "clerical conservatism" of the older regime...' (1968).

Fascism in the UK

The British Union of Fascists was the most influential fascist movement in Britain. It was set up in 1932 and gained a peak membership of 50,000. Its founder – **Oswald Mosley** (a former Conservative and Labour MP) – was interned during the 1939–45 war but re-emerged in 1948 as leader of the Union Movement. In 1967 the National Front was founded. Its candidates gained an average of 3.6 per cent of the vote in the 1970 General Election. It was succeeded by the British National Party (founded in 1983).

In summary, the key themes of the fascist ideology are: aggressive nationalism and a hatred of democracy.

GREEN IDEOLOGY

In his *A Green History of the World* (1991) Clive Ponting places the Green political agenda in a world-historical context. Two million years ago the first direct ancestors of humans emerged. Ten thousand years ago settled cultivation was introduced by the agricultural revolution. Since then the human population has increased from four million to around six billion. Greens reject the view that the present rate of pollution of the atmosphere and exploitation of national resources (including non-renewable resources such as water, soil, and forests) can be sustained. Many of the planet's natural ecosystems have been either severely disrupted or destroyed. Scientists warn that within the next 25 years between 1 and 10 per cent of all species will have disappeared because of human activity (there are an estimated 13 million species on the planet).

In the view of the Greens in Germany 'the world-wide ecological crisis worsens from day to day: natural resources become more scarce; chemical waste dumps are subjects of scandal after scandal; whole species of animals are exterminated; entire varieties of plants become extinct; rivers and oceans change slowly into sewers; and humans verge on spiritual and intellectual decay in the midst of a mature, industrial, consumer society'. As the 1997 *Green Party Manifesto* put it: 'We live on a planet of finite size but we use it as if it were a limitless source of resources and a free dustbin.'

The Green Party (formed in 1973) was first known as the People Party, then the Ecology Party, and was renamed the Green Party in 1985. Its most successful election performance was in 1989 when it gained 15 per cent of the vote in the European elections. In Germany, the Green activist **Petra Kelly** gained a wide public following and her Party became an important force in national politics. In the General Election of 1998 the Greens gained 6.7 per cent of the vote and 47 out of the 669 seats in the Bundestag. (In 1987 they gained 8.2 per cent of the vote).

Barry describes green political theory as 'the newest of all political theories'. It has been 'vilified from the left for being a "petty bourgeois" ideology with conservative, anti-progressive undertones, while from the right it has been criticised as propounding an anti-technological message and seeking to return society to a pre-modern state'. A central concern of green political theory is 'with the status of the non-human world and its treatment of humans'. 'Dark greens' subscribe to a 'deep ecology' position: 'nature should be seen as having intrinsic value and should be protected for its own sake and not simply because it is of benefit to human beings.' 'Light greens' subscribe to a 'shallow ecology' position: the primary concern should be 'the effect of ecological damage on human health and well being' (1998).

Environmentalism is a managerial approach to tackling environmental problems which believes they can be solved without fundamental changes in values or the economy. **Ecologism** calls for radical changes in our whole way of life. In 1972 **James Lovelock** formulated the ecological concept of **Gaia**: this sees the earth as a living entity which human beings are duty bound to protect. Every part of the earth – including plants and rocks as well as all living species – is interdependent on each other.

In summary, the key themes of the Green ideology are: the crisis for living species and the future of the planet posed by man's exploitative and destructive impact on the environment.

EXAMPLE OF A NEW IDEOLOGY: COMMUNITARIANISM

Amitai Etzioni (1993) has outlined the key themes of communitarianism.

- The name 'communitarian' was adopted 'to emphasise that the time has come to attend to our responsibilities to the conditions and elements we all share, to the community'.
- A new social, philosophical, and political map is needed: the division between Left and Right 'often no longer serves'.
- Faith in the political system has dropped. In 1991, 46 per cent of Americans believed that quite a few government officials were crooked compared with 30 per cent in the late 1950s.
- Poor parenting has made a major contribution to social problems such as drug abuse, gang warfare, and a poorly committed workforce. It has left individuals with 'a strong sense of entitlement and weak sense of responsibility'.
- For a transition period of a decade or so we should 'put a tight lid on the manufacturing of new rights. The incessant issuance of new rights, like the wholesale printing of currency, causes a massive inflation of rights that devalues their currency'.
- '"What is Communitarianism?" we are frequently asked. We are a social movement aiming at shoring up the moral, social, and political environment. Part change of heart, part renewal of social bonds, part reform of public life.'
- In order to strengthen the moral foundations of our society 'we start with the family ... second in line are the schools ... Third are the social webs that communities provide, in neighbourhoods, at work, and in ethnic clubs and associations, the webs that bind individuals, who would otherwise be on their own, into groups of people who care for one another and who help maintain a civic, social and moral order.'

Study point

Information on party policies and political movements is available on Richard Kimber's 'Political Science Resource' Site: http://www.psr.keele.ac.uk

POINTS OF EVALUATION

1 Conservatism underplays the social costs and injustices generated by large-scale inequalities in the distribution of wealth, income and power.
2 Liberalism continues to be deeply divided on the role of the State. For some liberals State intervention is a threat to liberty, for others it is a safeguard of liberty.
3 Socialism has still to devise a viable economic alternative to capitalism. While some socialists argue that the commanding heights of the economy should be brought under public (or workers') control, others believe they should be privately owned but be closely regulated by the State.
4 Communism has ignored the threat to liberty posed by concentrating both economic and political power in the hands of a revolutionary party. *Classocide* – the mass murder of individuals designated as belonging to a particular social class – has been practised in a number of communist States.
5 Nationalism is described by Tom Nairn as 'the modern Janus'. It has two very different faces: positively it is a source of belonging and identity, while negatively it is a source of irrational aggression towards outsiders.
6 Fascism repudiates concepts of individual liberty and democracy. *Genocide* – the mass murder of individuals designated as belonging to particular ethnic groups – has been practised by fascist States.
7 Green ideology tends to portray humans' impact on the environment in over-alarmist, apocalyptic and 'end of the world' terms.

Study point

The following quotations relate to definitions of conservatism, liberalism, socialism, communism, nationalism, fascism, and green ideology. Which is which?

1 *'The only freedom which deserves the name, is that of pursuing our own good in our own way, so long as we do not deprive others of theirs, or impede their efforts to obtain it.'*

2 *'The political outlook which springs from a desire to conserve existing things, held to be either good in themselves, or better than the likely alternatives, or at least safe, familiar, and the objects of trust and affection.'*

3 *'...denies that numbers, by the mere fact of being numbers, can direct human society; it denies that these numbers can govern by means of periodic consultations; it affirms also the fertilising, beneficent and unassailable inequality of men, who cannot be levelled through an extrinsic and mechanical process such as universal suffrage.'*

4 *'The right of individuals to choose the state to which they belong, that is, to establish territorial political structures corresponding to their consciousness of group identity...'*

5 *'Using the power of democratic politics to correct the persistent tendency of market forces to create ever-growing inequality.'*

6 *'A political doctrine, originating in the French Revolution, according to which human society can be organised on the basis of the common ownership of economic resources by the direct producers or workers.'*

7 *'It is concerned with generations yet unborn, with other species, and with the future of the planet.'*

Answers on page 135.

SUMMARY

- An ideology is an 'action-directing' cluster of ideas which is both descriptive and prescriptive.
- Marxists view ideology as a set of ideas which advance the interests of the dominant class.
- The working class has been seen as actively supporting a hegemonic ideology (Gramsci), as largely indifferent to ideology (Abercrombie), and as able to 'see through' ideology (Lukács).
- Intellectuals have been portrayed as self-interested members of a 'new class' (Gouldner) and as truth-seekers who are able to 'see through' ideology (Mannheim).
- In the 1960s theorists announced the 'end of ideology' and in the 1990s the 'end of history'. (The 'end' never quite arrives.)
- The leftwing–rightwing classification of ideologies originates in the French Revolution of 1789. Parties of the Left favour State intervention in order to bring about greater equality, while parties of the Right regard such intervention as a threat to property rights and personal liberty.
- Conservatism values stability, hierarchy, and entrepreneurial individualism.
- Liberalism values liberty and defence of individual rights.
- Socialism values equality and the redistribution of individual rights.
- Communism values the establishment of a society based on common ownership.
- Nationalism values the nation as the primary source of loyalty and identity.
- Fascism values the establishment of a dictatorial and ultra-nationalistic State.
- Greens value protection of living species and the environment.

Group work

1 Group one presents the case for conservatism. Group two presents the case for liberalism. Group three presents the case for socialism.
2 Interview members of local political parties. Ask them to outline the key components of their political ideology or core political beliefs.
3 A *Guardian*/ICM opinion poll based on a random sample of 1,120 adults aged 18 and over was carried out in October 1998. It asked: 'When people talk about politics, they sometimes talk about the left, the right and the centre. Where would you put yourself on this scale?' It found that 7 per cent of voters said they were 'Leftwing', 15 per cent 'Left of centre', 37 per cent 'Centre', 13 per cent 'Right of centre', and 5 per cent 'Rightwing'. Conduct a survey in your local area to see if there is a similar pattern of ideological affiliation.

Key Concepts activity

1 Define and explain the following terms: hegemony; false consciousness; the end of ideology thesis; the ideological state apparatus.
2 Distinguish between the following sets of terms: self-regarding and other-regarding actions; negative liberty and positive liberty; civic nationalism and ethnic nationalism; environmentalism and ecologism.

Practice questions

1 'British politics continue to be dominated by a division between leftwing and rightwing ideologies.' Discuss.
2 'All ideologies seek to advance the sectional interests of a particular social group.' Explain and discuss.
3 Assess the view that the working class in the UK is a victim of false consciousness.
4 'Nor is it the case that all commitment to the dominant social order involves some sort of delusion. Someone might have a perfectly adequate understanding of the mechanisms of capitalist exploitation, but conclude that this kind of society, while unjust and oppressive, is on the whole preferable to any likely alternative.' (Terry Eagleton). Discuss with reference to the concept of a *dominant ideology*.

Coursework Suggestions

1 There has been a resurgence of ideological movements in recent decades. *Republican nationalism* and *Protestant loyalism* have dominated the politics of

Northern Ireland. *Christian Evangelicalism* emerged in the USA in the late 1970s and has considerable influence inside the Republican Party. *Communitarianism* – an anti-individualistic ideology which stresses the importance of community and personal responsibility – has gained a considerable following. *Islamism* – a new radical politics of religious activism – achieved State power during the Iranian revolution of 1979 and is an important force in the Muslim world. Make a case study of one ideology. Examine its key ideas and beliefs, the social characteristics of its supporters, and the factors which contributed to its emergence.

2 Is there a 'dominant ideology' in Britain which is supported by a majority of the population? (Interviews could be conducted with a random sample of individuals to explore their core political beliefs and values.)

5

PRESSURE GROUPS AND PUBLIC POLICY

Introduction

THIS CHAPTER EXAMINES pressure groups and the impact they have on public policy. Pressure groups are organised bodies which seek to influence decision-making in order to protect interests and/or promote causes. Insider groups – unlike outsider groups – are consulted by governments on a regular basis. Some pressure groups have ideological affiliations with Old Social Movements while others have ideological affiliations with New Social Movements. In the view of pluralist theorists the United Kingdom is a polyarchal democracy in which public policy is influenced by numerous pressure groups. But neo-pluralist theorists see the UK as a deformed polyarchy because some pressure groups are more successful in influencing public policy than others. Marxist theorists believe that the most effective pressure groups are those which represent the interests of private capital. New Right theorists are also critical of pressure group politics and believe it can lead to economic stagnation and political crisis. In the view of feminist theorists pressure group politics operate on the basis of a male-dominated political agenda.

PRESSURE GROUPS

The central aim of pressure group organisations is to influence public policy. Public policy is formulated by governments – the national government, European Union government, or local government. Public policy includes decisions on public expenditure and taxation: how much should be spent on education, the armed forces, and State pensions? How much income tax and council tax should people pay? Should those with high incomes pay significantly more tax than those on low incomes? Public policy includes decisions on transport: should the use of

Table 4: *Theorists, concepts and issues in this chapter*		
KEY THEORISTS	KEY CONCEPTS	KEY ISSUES
Bentley (1870–1957)	Pressure groups	• Seek to influence public policy
Finer (1915–93) Stewart (b. 1929)	Protective groups	• Based on shared interests
Finer, Stewart	Promotional groups	• Based on shared beliefs
Grant	Outsider groups	• Excluded from official consultation process
Grant	Outsider groups	• Excluded from official consultation process
Saint-Simon (1760–1825)	Social movements	• Alliances for or against social change
Dahl (b. 1915)	Pluralist theory	• Polyarchal Democracy
Dahl	Neo-Pluralist theory	• Deformed Polyarchy
Miliband, Poulantzas (1936–1979)	Marxist theory	• Public policy shaped by the interests of capital
Brittan (b. 1939)	New right	• Pressure groups 'over-load' the political system
Barrett (b. 1949)	Feminist	• Public policy shaped by patriarchy

motor cars in cities be discouraged? Should more motorways be built? Public policy also includes foreign policy issues of peace and war.

Pressure groups – unlike political parties – seek to influence Government but do not contest elections and seek to become the Government. The pioneer theorist of the study of pressure groups was **Arthur Bentley** who wrote *The Process of Government* (1904). This was based on empirical investigations of the decision-making process in Chicago and the State of Illinois. Bentley saw pressure group activity as *the* key determinant of public policy. In the UK, the first major studies of pressure groups were by **S. E. Finer** – *Anonymous Empire* (1958) and **J. D. Stewart** – *British Pressure Groups* (1958).

HISTORY OF PRESSURE GROUPS

Pressure group activity is not new. During the eighteenth and nineteenth centuries protective groups (such as canal and railway companies) and promotional groups (such as the Anti-Slavery Society and the Anti-Corn Law League) were politically influential. A protective pressure group – the trade union movement – played a key role in establishing the Labour Party. Pressure group activity increased in the postwar decades. The Consumers' Association was founded in 1957, the Child Poverty Action Group in 1965, and Shelter in 1966. Baggott (1995) sees the underlying political culture as favouring the growth of pressure group politics.

> *'The continued decline of class politics, the growing importance of single issues, particularly quality of life issues, and the growing assertiveness of the public have all been reflected in increased participation in pressure groups.'*

Factors which have led to the growth in pressure group activity include:

1 more extensive government intervention in the economy
2 the expansion of the welfare state
3 the growth in the size and influence of the new middle class
4 the increased complexity of modern society
5 the highlighting of issues by the mass media.

TYPES OF PRESSURE GROUP

The aim of **protective** groups (sometimes referred to as **sectional**, **interest** or **defensive** groups) is to represent specific group interests. The aim of **promotional** groups (sometimes referred to as **cause** or **attitude** groups) is to represent specific beliefs or viewpoints.

THE CAMPAIGN FOR NUCLEAR DISARMAMENT (CND) WAS FOUNDED IN 1958. IT IS AN EXAMPLE OF A PROMOTIONAL PRESSURE GROUP. ESCALATING TENSIONS BETWEEN THE NUCLEAR SUPERPOWERS LED TO A DRAMATIC INCREASE IN ITS MEMBERSHIP FROM AROUND 2,000 IN 1979 TO 100,000 IN 1981 (WHEN THIS PHOTOGRAPH WAS TAKEN).

Pressure groups have been subdivided into:

1 **Ad Hoc** (special purpose) groups which disappear once their goals have been achieved. (The term **fire-brigade groups** refers to pressure groups which are formed spontaneously to protest against a new proposal.)
2 **Ideas** groups whose members do not derive any financial gains from the goals pursued by the organisation.
3 **Interest** groups which represent the interests of either producers or consumers.
4 **Self-help** groups deal with the immediate concerns of their members (eg Alcoholics Anonymous).
5 **Peak groups** are organisations such as the Trades Union Congress (TUC) or Confederation of British Industry (CBI) which speak for a set of interests.
6 **Latent groups** exist where individuals with common interests have no formal organisations to speak for them (eg Claimants of State benefits before Claimants' Unions were formed; homeless people before Shelter was formed).
7 **Political cause groups** seek to change the structure of the political system (eg Charter 88 campaigns for a Bill of Rights, a fair electoral system, freedom of information, a democratic second chamber, a reformed judiciary, and a written constitution).

Study point

- The website for the Trade Union Congress is: www.tuc.org.uk
- The website for the Confederation of British Industry is: www.cbi.org.uk

PRESSURE GROUP ACTIVITY

Targets and Focal Points of pressure group activity:

1 The Government, the civil service, executive institutions of the European Union, and quangos (quasi-autonomous non-governmental organisations such as health authorities).
2 Legislators (Members of Parliament at Westminster and Members of the European Parliament in Brussels and Strasbourg).
3 Public Opinion.

Pressure in the European Union

EU policy can be influenced by:

- *The direct route*: making contact with European Union institutions in Brussels.
- *The indirect route*: making contact with government departments in Whitehall in order to change the bargaining position taken by the British Government in the Council of Ministers.

Study point

The European Union has become increasingly important as a focal point of pressure group activity.

The European Union's website address is: http://europa.eu.int/

Scroll down and click on 'Welcome'.

PRESSURE GROUPS AND GOVERNMENT

- Some pressure groups have a 'low profile' and rely on behind-the-scenes contacts. Others have a 'high profile' and make regular use of the mass media.
- **Policy communities** consist of networks of contacts between government departments and leading pressure groups in specific issue areas.
- **The policy agenda** consists of the issues being actively examined at any one time.
- Pressure groups with **insider status** are represented on official advisory committees and are regularly consulted by Government. Successful pressure groups will be able to influence the contents of **Green Papers** (consultative documents published by the government) and **White Papers** (which announce government policy proposals).
- **Outsider groups** lack credibility with Government and are not included in the process of official consultation. They can be subdivided into three categories:
  1. potential insider groups
  2. outsider groups by necessity (which have insufficient political knowledge and skills to be considered for insider status)
  3. ideological outsider groups (which do not believe that change can be achieved within the existing political system).
- The distinction between insider and outsider groups is a fluid one: some outsider groups gain 'promotion' to insider status, and some insider groups are 'relegated' to outsider status.
- **Thresholder groups** oscillate between using insider and outsider strategies (eg trade unions and small businessmen's groups).
- Many pressure groups use **political brokers** – individuals with inside knowledge of the corridors of power. Some pressure groups rely on low-profile methods: meetings are held with civil servants and ministers behind closed doors. Other pressure groups favour high-profile methods: campaigns are run in the media, and demonstrations and direct action protests may be organised.
- The campaign in the 1950s and 1960s to abolish the death penalty used *both* behind-the-scenes lobbying *and* public campaigning. One group – the Howard

League for Penal Reform – concentrated on winning over members of key elites (eg editors of quality newspapers) to the abolitionist case. Another group – the National Campaign for the Abolition of the Death Penalty – organised well publicised meetings, vigils, and petitions in order to reduce public support for the death penalty. Pressure groups often draw up a two-phase strategy: first a behind-the-scenes approach is used and if this fails a public campaign is launched.

Activity

In 1998 Barry Horne, a prisoner and Animal Rights activist, went on a 68 day hunger strike. He wanted the government to set up a Royal Commission on vivisection. The Labour Party had made no commitment to establish a Royal Commission in its election manifesto, although it did produce pre-election 'Life for Animals' posters. In response to Horne's campaign a Home Office spokesperson declared: 'we are not prepared to give in to blackmail.' In small groups discuss:

1 The arguments for and against the Government's stance on this issue.
2 The arguments for and against using hunger strikes as a method of applying pressure on Governments.

POINTS OF EVALUATION

Pressure group success and failure depends on such factors as:

1 organisational resources and political or media skills
2 size and social composition of membership (including whether sizeable numbers of the government's own potential supporters are members)
3 possession of insider or outsider status
4 degree or economic or strategic power
5 whether it is opposed by other pressure groups
6 extent of public support and legitimacy (teachers' groups will expect to gain a better hearing than groups representing ex-criminals)
7 ideological sympathies and electoral strategies of the Government.

METHODS OF PRESSURE GROUPS

LOBBYING

In recent years **lobbying agencies** have become more influential. These act as intermediaries or 'middle men' between pressure groups and Government. In the

USA (unlike in the UK) professional lobbyists must be registered. Many MPs are employed as consultants by lobbying agencies. In the UK in 1994 there was a 'cash for questions' scandal involving two government ministers, and ethical standards in public life became a major political issue. The 1998 *Neill Report* declared that 'many members of the public believe that the policies of the major political parties have been influenced by large donors…'. It recommended that a ban should be imposed on all foreign donations to Parties, and that donations to Parties of £5,000 or more nationally or £1,000 locally should be made public.

Activity

In small groups outline arguments for and against MPs acting as paid political consultants for lobbying agencies.

CAMPAIGNS

In local campaigns pressure group tactics include:

- lobbying local councillors, MPs and MEPs
- running well publicised meetings with 'star' speakers
- recruiting members, raising funds, and developing a solid organisational base
- gaining media coverage on radio, regional television, and in local newspapers
- producing leaflets, newsletters, and conducting research
- forming 'coalitions' with sympathetic organisations
- Political entrepreneurs – energetic and dynamic activists – can play a key role.

Community politics

The aim of community politics is to mobilise people into politics through:

- direct action and setting up locally-based organisations
- responding to the needs of the poorest groups in society (these, it is felt, are ignored by the established political institutions)
- In *Community Politics* (1976) Peter Hain, now a government minister, emphasised the need to cultivate 'the *habit* of participation'.
- Community politics 'involves a willingness to take direct action... it is a strategy of change from the bottom up rather than the top down'.

SOCIAL MOVEMENTS

These consist of 'any broad alliance of people who are associated in seeking to effect or to block an aspect of social change within a society' – *Collins Dictionary of Sociology* (1995). The term was first used by **Saint-Simon** to refer to movements of social protest. **Old Social Movements** (OSMs) tend to have a working class following and focus on mainly economic issues (eg the trade union movement). Organisational structures are often formal and centralised. **New Social Movements** (NSMs) tend to have a new middle class following and focus on post-materialist issues, such as quality of life, individual freedom, and self-expression, (eg the ecological movement). They have decentralised structures and stress participatory styles of decision-making.

POINTS OF EVALUATION

Jordan and Maloney (1997) contrast a *pressure group perspective* – which focuses on the relationships of groups to the political system – with a *social movement perspective* – which focuses on lack of hierarchy and formal organisation. New social movements express political frustration and discontent through loose groupings or configurations rather than through the bureaucratic structures. They have a more loose knit and open framework than political parties. (Justice, an anti-road building group, calls itself a 'disorganisation'.) They also have a wider agenda of issues than most pressure groups.

PROTESTS AND DEMONSTRATIONS

Some case studies

In *Demonstrations and Communication: A Case Study* (1970) **J. Halloran** documents a demonstration in Trafalgar Square in 1961 which represented a turning point in the postwar history of political demonstrations. A protest rally was organised by the Committee of One Hundred (a civil disobedience splinter group associated with the Campaign for Nuclear Disarmament). 1,314 people were arrested. This incident 'marked a new phase in the relationship between police and demonstrators'. Tougher policing methods (such as snatch squads and use of riot shields) began to be used.

J. Brewer in *The Police, Public Order and the State* (1988) describes how, during the 1980s, police-society relations deteriorated. A minority of demonstrators used violence against the police, and on a number of occasions the police employed riot squad tactics. 'A litany of names charts the changes in police strategy: Grunwick, Southall, St. Paul's, Brixton, Toxteth, Warrington, Orgreave, Stonehenge, Handsworth, Broadwater Farm, Wapping ...'

David Waddington et al in *Flashpoints. Studies in public disorder* (1989) examine a number of examples of public order breakdown.

1 During the 1979 General Election campaign the National Front declared its intention to hold a meeting in Southall (an area with a large Asian population). A sit-in protest was organised outside the Town Hall. This was forcibly dispersed by the police and one demonstrator – Blaire Peach – was killed.

2 In 1984 (during the miners' strike of 1984–5) members of the National Union of Miners (NUM) began picketing the Orgreave coke works. They hoped to repeat the success of a mass picket at Saltley in 1972 which had led to an NUM strike victory. The authorities regarded Orgreave as a showdown with the miners. Snatch squads and mounted police were used, the mass picket was broken, and the strike was eventually defeated.

Darren Hoad (1998) points to the revival in direct action that has taken place in recent years, despite the 1994 Criminal Justice and Public Order Act attempting to subject political protest to tighter regulation and control. 'In the environmental movement there is a wide range of groups whose main mode of political activity is rooted in direct action eg Greenpeace, Earth First!, Critical Mass, Reclaim the Streets, the roads protest movement and the Campaign Against the Second Runway at Manchester Airport (CAR2), Protests against live animal exports at Brightlingsea, the actions at Newbury, Twyford Down, Fairmile and the campaign against the M11 link road in London…'

Points to Note

- The concept of the **rule of law** is central to democratic theory. This holds that no one is above the law, and all citizens (including members of the government and officers of the State) must act in accordance with the law.
- **Direct action** is a form of political action which operates outside the formal political process. It consists of a range of activities that are 'demonstrative, obstructive, publicity seeking, increasingly illegal and sometimes violent' (Hoad, 1998). Recent examples of direct action include anti-traffic protesters holding a party in the middle of Piccadilly Circus in order to bring traffic to a halt; building tunnels and occupying houses and trees in order to halt the construction of new motorways; disabled groups holding sit-down protests near Downing Street.

Activity

In small groups discuss whether there are any circumstances in which individuals in democratic societies such as the UK would be justified in breaking the law.

THEORIES OF PRESSURE GROUP INFLUENCE

Pluralist

The state is seen as performing a politically neutral 'umpire' role. The decision-making process in what Dahl describes as 'modern, dynamic, pluralist (MDP) society' is shaped by multiple pressure, and ordinary citizens have an effective say in politics.

- Pressure groups complement the role of political parties. They provide a vehicle for political activity between elections; act as a voice for minority opinion; increase levels of political awareness; enable citizens to express the intensity of their views on specific issues; and keep elected representatives in touch with public opinion. In McKenzie's view pressure groups are a force for democracy and enable citizens to 'advise, cajole, and warn [the authorities] regarding the policies they should adopt' (1963).
- According to the **convergence thesis** all industrial societies, whatever their ideologies, come to resemble each other (both in terms of social structure and political process). An 'iron law of pluralism' is at work. Thus in the post-1953 years government policy in the Soviet Union was increasingly shaped by bargaining and compromises between different pressure groups. A variety of interests (eg the military, industrial managers, the Party apparatus, the media, and academics) influenced decision-making in this one-party state.
- Pressure group activity and a tradition of representative democracy ensures that societies like the United Kingdom are **polyarchal democracies** in which the many rule.

Neo-pluralist

Some pressure groups are able to exert far more influence on the decision-making process than others. In his later writings Dahl accepts that inequalities in citizens' 'political resources, in their strategic positions, and in their overt and implicit bargaining power are sufficiently great even in democratic orders to lend plausibility to theories of minority domination' (1989).

- Some protective groups (such as trans-national corporations like Rupert Murdoch's News International) possess formidable economic muscle and carry more 'clout' with governments than promotional groups (even ones with large memberships and substantial public support).
- Neo-pluralist theory takes a more *analytical* stance than orthodox pluralist theory. It is concerned with describing how things *are* rather than with making normative prescriptions about how things *should* be. Societies like the UK are viewed as **deformed polyarchies** in which the democratic process is less than perfect and some groups have far more of a say over decision-making than others.

Marxist

The State is seen as directly supporting the interests of organised business: it is 'the executive committee of the bourgeoisie'. In the Marxist view '*the most well-organised group in Britain is the City of London*, that is, the commercial banks (such as NatWest), merchant banks (Hill Samuel), insurance companies (Guardian Royal Exchange), pension funds, finance houses, the Stock Exchange, foreign currency dealers, and the Bank of England' (Abercrombie and Warde, 1994).

Neo-Marxist

Neo-Marxist interpretations of the relationship between economic and political power focus on:

1 The relative autonomy (partial independence) of the State. It acts in the interests of private capital – but does not simply do what the representatives of private capital tell it to do. The State has to take a long-term view of what is in the interests of business rather than being swayed by the short-term interests of particular groups.
2 The existence of a power bloc. This is made up of an alliance of business-dominated groups which agree on a shared political programme. They then apply pressure on the state to ensure that it is implemented.
3 The State as an **instrumental** mechanism. It is a means by which individuals from privileged social backgrounds advance their own interests. They voluntaristically choose to use the State apparatus as an instrument to further sectional advantage.
4 The State as a **structural** mechanism. Economic imperatives – the need to increase profits and accumulate wealth – compel government ministers and civil servants to administer policies which favour the interests of private capital. The State forms an integral part of a broader politico-economic system and has only a limited autonomy. Rather than being used *by* individuals it is the State which *uses* individuals.
5 The hegemonic character of the State. It performs a cultural leadership role and seeks to persuade subordinate social classes to accept the dominant ideology. The State not only steers the economic order but also stabilises the social order.
6 The possibility of a legitimisation crisis if economic policies fail. A prolonged fiscal shortfall (taxation revenue being insufficient to fund public expenditure) would lead to massive cuts in expenditure on health, education and welfare. Public confidence in the political system might then collapse.

New Right

The danger of pressure group activity is that it might 'over-load' the political system and thereby bring about 'hyper-pluralism' and 'ungovernability'. Pluralists celebrate the proliferation of pressure groups as evidence of the vitality of democracy. But new right theorists believe this could lead to economic collapse and a legitimisation crisis. In the view of **Samuel Brittan** 'interest groups do not merely reduce the national income when they become embedded in the political process. They embody rival claims which more than exhaust the national product and threaten the survival of liberal democracy itself.'

The New Right in the UK

New Right theorists claim that Britain in the late 1970s was in a situation of **pluralist stagnation** – of political and economic paralysis – because of the over-readiness of government to comply with pressure group demands.

In the 1980s a number of **think-tanks** supported the New Right analysis. Think-tanks are research organisations which specialise in floating new political ideas and formulating innovative policy proposals. Think-tanks which were particularly influential in the 1980s included the Institute of Economic Affairs (set up in 1955), the Centre for Policy Studies (1974), and the Adam Smith Institute (1981). They acted as 'anti-pressure group pressure groups' and tried to persuade governments to ignore pressure group demands.

Margaret Thatcher (Prime Minister from 1979–90) was receptive to the monetarist analysis put forward by the New Right. This claimed that high levels of public expenditure, high levels of taxation and borrowing, inflation (over 24 per cent in 1975), and economic stagnation were all causally linked to each other. The more governments try to 'spend their way' out of problems and placate pressure group demands, the more serious the crisis becomes. Only by cutting through the 'Gordian's knot' of pressure group politics and ending the postwar 'consensus' of a mixed economy and high public spending could stability be restored.

In the 1980s there was a major shift in the stance towards pressure groups taken by government. Neo-corporatist tripartite institutions such as the National Economic Development Council (NEDC) were downgraded. (In 1992 NEDC was finally abolished.) A number of sectional interests (such as opticians and solicitors) were exposed to greater competition. The power of trade unions was drastically curtailed.

Feminist

The State is viewed as a patriarchal institution which furthers the cause of male domination and serves the interests of men rather than women. Both the input of pressure group activity and the output of government policy reflect the priorities of a male-based agenda.

- All the key sectors of the State apparatus – the cabinet, the higher ranks of the civil service, the judiciary, and the military – are overwhelmingly staffed by men. In the 1997 General Election only 120 of the 659 MPs elected to the House of Commons were female.
- Until 1918 women were not even allowed to stand for election to Parliament. They were excluded from the public sphere of political power as well as being subjected to male domination in the private sphere of the household.
- 'First wave' feminism achieved political and legal equality (New Zealand in 1893 was the first country in which women gained the vote). The goal of 'second wave' feminism was to gain social and economic equality. It has only achieved partial success: women continue to be disproportionately represented in part-time and low-paid employment, have lower full-time earnings than men, carry out the bulk of housework and child care responsibilities, and are subjected to domestic violence and sexual harassment.

- On a whole range of policy issues (eg child care, welfare benefit regulations, abortion, pornography, images used in advertising, and equal opportunities in the workplace) female interests have been marginalised or simply ignored. **Michelle Barrett** believes that 'elements of male domination' are 'incorporated into the particular family-household system that the State has supported and structured …' (1980).
- **Liberal feminism** claims that it is possible to eliminate the patriarchal character of the State by a process of piecemeal reform. Real gains were achieved by the 1970 Equal Pay Act and the 1975 Sex Discrimination Act. Females are now outperforming males in most areas of educational attainment, and the cumulative impact of such cultural change will erode gender-based power inequalities.
- **Socialist feminism** claims that the patriarchal character of the State will only disappear once capitalism is replaced by a non-exploitative socio-economic system. In our society women constitute a 'sex-class' – the most exploited sector of the working-class. Capitalism deliberately fosters gender divisions, uses sexuality to sell commodities and make profit, and confines large numbers of women to unpaid domestic work in the home and/or low pay outside the home.
- **Radical feminism** claims that the patriarchal character of the State has deep ideological roots and will not be removed by either incremental step-by-step reforms or by revolution (which will, if history is any guide, be led by patriarchal males)!
- Pressure groups – like the governments they seek to influence – are overwhelmingly male-dominated bodies. Public policy is formed inside patriarchal decision-making structures which give priority to the interests of the male minority of the population.

Activity

Check the national and local press for a week. Write to your local MP, MEP, councillors or others in decision-making positions. What examples can you obtain of public policy being influenced by pressure group activity?

POINTS OF EVALUATION

1 Pluralists exaggerate the openness and democratic responsiveness of the political system. Some groups (eg trans-national corporations or strategically placed trade unions) exert more influence than others. The interests of many ordinary citizens are ignored.

2 Neo-pluralists use the term *deformed polyarchal democracy*. But in some political systems deformations – the disproportionate influence exerted by powerful groups – are so great that a political system can no longer be described as democratic.
3 Marxists assume that economic power brings with it political power and that organised business has a decisive influence on government policy. But to see the State as a puppet pulled by the strings of private capital is to engage in a crude form of economic determinism and ignore the autonomy of politics.
4 In the early 1980s the UK government introduced deflationary economic policies which were inspired by the New Right. They were (at least in the short-term) a failure: unemployment increased by 1.4 million between 1979 and 1981, and manufacturing output fell by 15 per cent in 1980. If governments are to retain democratic consent they must respond to legitimate pressure group demands. Rather than being a source of instability, high levels of public expenditure can promote economic prosperity and social cohesion.
5 Changes have taken place in the gender composition of key institutions which call into question the concept of the Patriarchal State. Females occupy (or have recently occupied) important positions in MI5, the Crown Prosecution Service, the Parliamentary Commissioner for Standards, the Bank of England, regulatory agencies, and the Monarchy. Both the Speaker of the House of Commons and the Leader of the House of Lords (as well as a former Prime Minister) are female. In 1918, one female was elected to the House of Commons compared with 120 in 1997. Rosemary Pringle and Sophie Watson (in Barrett and Phillips, 1992) write that earlier feminist accounts of the State over-emphasised its effectiveness in reproducing patriarchal relationships. The State is now seen as 'a by-product of political struggles' rather than 'a unified structure'.

Study point

The following are: four pressure groups – a protective group, a promotional group, an ideological outsider group, and a peak group – and three left-of-centre think-tanks. Which is which?

1 Animal Liberation Front
2 Fabian Society
3 Confederation of British Industry (CBI)
4 National Association of Teachers in Further and Higher Education (NATFHE)
5 Institute for Public Policy Research
6 Society for the Protection of Unborn Children
7 Demos.

Answers on page 135.

Study point

The Demos think-tank website is: http://www.demos.co.uk

PRESSURE GROUPS AND THE STATE

In *The Question of UK Decline. The Economy, State and Society* (1994) David Coates investigates the relationships between pressure groups and the State, and the impact these can have on economic growth. Compared with other industrial societies (especially the USA, Germany and Japan) the UK has underperformed economically since the 1950s. Its manufacturing sector has been slow to modernise and has failed to maintain its competitive position.

Explanations for the UK's relative economic decline include:

1 *The impact of an overactive State*: pressure group activity and consensus politics led to high levels of taxation and public expenditure. By 1975, 7.2 million people were employed in the public sector. There were too many government officials, too few producers, and investment in the private sector was 'squeezed out' by State spending. The State gave in to pressure groups demands, government spending rose, and the economy suffered.
2 *The impact of an underactive State*: in economically successful industrial societies the State has played a key role in encouraging economic growth and funding investment in new industries (eg electronics in Japan, chemicals in Germany, information technology in the USA). But in the UK the State was not 'subject to any prolonged pressure from organised business for active industrial intervention' and government did little to help modernise the economy. If there had been more pressure from UK companies for State assistance the result would have been higher levels of investment and more economic growth. Ordinary citizens would have eventually benefited from higher living standards.

Activity

In small groups discuss the advantages of:

1 the State forming a *close* relationship with organised business.
2 the State having a more *distant* relationship with organised business.

6

POLITICAL PARTICIPATION AND VOTING BEHAVIOUR

Introduction

THIS CHAPTER EXAMINES various forms of political participation including voting in election and referendums. Political participation ranges from engaging in informal political discussion to taking part in the formal decision-making processes of government or joining in revolutions which overthrow governments. Both participation and non-participation in politics are influenced by social, economic, life cycle, and psychological factors, and by the impact of government policies which seek to encourage or discourage participation. Leading theories of voting behaviour focus on the influence of social class, political socialisation, 'rational' choice, embourgeoisement, sectoral cleavages, class dealignment, and the interaction between politics and social structure.

POLITICAL PARTICIPATION

In the political tradition stemming from the Greek city states and the Roman republic, citizenship has meant involvement in public affairs by those who hold the rights of citizens: to take part in public debate and, directly or indirectly, in shaping the laws and decisions of a state'

Report of the Advisory Group on Education for Citizenship and the Teaching of Democracy in Schools (1998)

Table 5: *Theorists, concepts and issues in this chapter*		
KEY THEORISTS	KEY CONCEPTS	KEY ISSUES
Greek and Roman philosophers	Political participation	• Voluntarily taking part in politics is a civic obligation
Parry and Moyser	Determinants of participation	• Class, gender, ethnicity, age, location, personality
Rousseau (1712–78), Mill (1806–73)	Democracy	• Desirability of participation
McKenzie and Silver	Deviant voting	• Working-class conservatism
Butler (b.1924) and Stokes	Political socialisation	• Influence of family background
Downs	Rational Choice Theory	• Maximisation of self-interest
Zweig	Embourgeoisment	• Labour Party working-class support eroded by affluence
Dunleavy (b. 1952) and Husbands	Sectoral cleavages	• New fault line in politics
Crewe (b. 1945), Denver	Class dealignment	• Weakening of relationship between class and voting
Heath (b. 1942)	Interactionist Theory	• Parties and social structure both influence voting

There are two ways in which individuals can participate in the political life of their society:

1 by voluntary participation
2 by non-voluntary participation.

VOLUNTARY PARTICIPATION

This type of involvement covers the following activities:

1 engaging in informal political discussions
2 attending political meetings
3 joining demonstrations, distributing political leaflets, or organising petitions
4 becoming an active member of a political party or pressure group
5 seeking election to a local council, a national assembly, the UK parliament, or the European Parliament
6 canvassing members of the public to vote in a particular way or support a particular cause

STUDENT RIOTS IN PARIS, 1968

7 writing letters on political issues to government ministers, elected representatives, or newspapers
8 voting in elections
9 taking part in non-violent forms of direct action (such as sit-down protests in public places)
10 engaging in political violence (as has happened in Northern Ireland)
11 participating in a revolution.

Activity

In small groups list the various forms of political participation you have engaged in over the last six months. How would you characterise your political involvement (eg activist, sporadic activist or apathetic)? Contrast your involvement in other organisations or clubs. Account for the differences.

NON-VOLUNTARY POLITICAL PARTICIPATION

This occurs when:

- citizens in a totalitarian state are directed to attend a political rally.
- citizens are forced to vote for a single party under pain of sanctions.

PARTICIPATION AND DEMOCRACY

Jean-Jacques Rousseau and **John Stuart Mill** saw political participation as a vital component of democracy. In Mill's view it is only through taking part in political debate – in 'the collision of adverse opinions' – that 'the truth has any chance of being supplied'. Political participation is seen as improving the quality of decision-making, raising levels of political education, meeting the responsibilities of citizenship, and subjecting holders of political office to control and accountability. The American sociologist **Richard Sennett** believes there has been a sharp decline in involvement in civic and public life. People have withdrawn into claustrophobic private lives, into 'the tyrannies of intimacy' (1977).

POINTS OF EVALUATION

1 Some theorists reject the view that political participation is essential in democratic society.

> *'Much of the division on the subject comes down to a fundamental value judgement about the place of politics in a fulfilled human life. Is political action the highest possible calling or is it just sitting in boring meetings?'*
>
> *The Concise Oxford Dictionary of Politics (1996)*

2 Pluralists see high levels of political participation as a sign of crisis extremism. If a political system is working well, a high proportion of the population will be content – and politically apathetic.

Participation in Parties and Pressure Groups

Over recent decades there has been a decline in participation in political parties.

Table 6: *Membership of political parties in 1950 and 1998*

YEAR	MEMBERSHIP OF POLITICAL PARTIES
1950	3 million
1998	1 million

Table 7: *Membership of the Labour and Conservative Parties in 1950 and 1998*

Year	Labour	Conservative
1953	1.0 million	2.8 million
1998	392,000	350,000
Average age of members in the 1990s	48	62

In 1989 only 1.6 per cent of the population of the UK were members of political parties. This compared with 2.3 per cent in Germany, 7.4 per cent in Italy, and 14.5 per cent in Sweden. The marginalisation of the grass roots membership of political parties has been explained in terms of the expansion of the media's role in communicating between political elites and voters; parties' increased reliance on experts (rather than amateur party members) for policy advice; and the development of direct mail which enables parties to bypass members in campaigning and fund-raising (Whiteley et al, 1994).

- During election campaigns only 1 per cent of the electorate engages in voluntary work for political parties (or some 500 workers per constituency).
- Attendance at public meetings has declined. In recent General Elections only around 3 per cent of electors said they had attended a political meeting. Today's electors connect with elections through television rather than 'live' events.
- While membership of political parties has declined, membership of pressure groups has increased. Over 60 per cent of adults belong to at least one pressure group. The total membership of environmental pressure groups alone is now over 4.5 million. Membership of Friends of the Earth increased from 1,000 in 1971 to 120,000 in 1993. Greenpeace has over 410,00 members, and the Royal Society for the Protection of Birds over 850,000 members. Social attitudes surveys have found that individuals in the 1990s say they are more prepared to engage in political action than they were in the 1960s.
- Survey research indicates that there has been a decline in public confidence in the political system. An ICM poll commissioned by Channel 4 in 1994 found that only 61 per cent of the public regarded the UK as a 'democratic country' (compared with 69 per cent in 1969). Twenty per cent believed that the UK was becoming less democratic (against 12 per cent who thought democracy was on the increase). Only 16 per cent believed that ordinary voters had much power to influence government policies between elections, while 26 per cent believed they has no influence at all. Similar trends are evident in the USA. In 1964 76 per cent of the public said they trusted the government in Washington to do the right thing 'all' or 'most' of the time. In 1994 the proportion had dropped to 25 per cent.

Factors affecting participation

Political Participation is related to:

1. *Social class*: ownership of wealth, a high income, and experience of higher education are positively associated with political participation. This is reflected in the composition of the House of Commons. In 1997, 81 per cent of Conservative MPs and 66 per cent of Labour MPs had attended university. Only 13 per cent of Labour MPs (54 in number) came from manual working class backgrounds – the lowest proportion ever. (The number of MPs who were Old Etonians (18) was also at an all time low.)
2. *Gender*: of the 659 MPs elected to the House of Commons in 1997, 539 were male. The 120 female MPs represented a doubling of the 1992 figure. Many women take responsibility for child care at a time when men are building their political careers.
3. *Age*: young people are less likely to be active in political parties and pressure groups than older people (although they are more likely to engage in direct action politics). This is reflected in the House of Commons. In 1997, the average age of Labour and Conservative MPs was 49.8. In the early 1990s only 5 per cent of Conservative Party members were aged under 35.
4. *Ethnicity*: electoral turn-out is high amongst members of the Jewish community and low amongst members of the Afro-Caribbean community. In the 1997 General Election there were only 42 major party candidates who came from ethnic minority backgrounds. Less than 2 per cent of MPs (9 in total) came from Afro-Caribbean or Asian backgrounds. There were 20 Jewish MPs.
5. *Residential location*: participation rates in rural locations are lower than those in urban locations (inner-city areas, which have a high turnover of population, are an exception). The longer an individual is a resident of a particular area the more likely s/he is to participate in politics.
6. *Socialisation experiences and personality factors*: outgoing and extroverted individuals are more likely to be politically active, especially if they were encouraged to take part in decision-making in the family home during childhood. A key factor in political participation is a sense of political efficacy – an individual's feeling that he or she is able to influence politics and be effective. Many political activists are born into politically active families.

Studies of Participation

Parry and **Moyser** use a 'resource model' to account for different levels of political participation. They define 'resources' as 'material wealth, educationally-based skills, and membership of organisations such as political parties, trade unions and voluntary groups'.

- Survey research reveals that political participation increases with wealth – direct action being the one exception: 'It is the poor who protest, not the wealthy'. Graduates have high levels of participation while those with no qualifications have low levels. Group affiliation – belonging to voluntary associations – is 'amongst the most powerful predictors of participation' in politics.

- A 'life-cycle effect' leads to participation peaking in middle age.
- Traditionally men have been more politically active than women, but the gender gap has narrowed significantly. Single women are more active than single men, and women are more likely to vote than men.

Parry, **Moyser**, and **Day** conducted a survey in 1985 of 1,578 respondents throughout Britain (1991). They found that 1.5 per cent of the adult population in Britain were 'complete activists' for whom politics is a central life interest, and 3.5 per cent had canvassed on behalf of a political party. Around half were 'just voters', while just over a quarter of the population took no part in political activity at all (not even voting).

- The survey included a list of 23 different political actions (eg contacting an MP, attending a protest meeting, voting in a local election). Only 23 per cent of those interviewed has performed more than four of these actions over the previous five years.
- Only a quarter if the population engaged in substantial political activity. Those who are 'almost inactive' and 'just voters' together make up three out of every four citizens.

Activity

Surveys have found that around 6 per cent of the population say they are very interested in politics, and 11 per cent discuss politics frequently. Political activists have been defined as those who take part in at least 5 out of 10 political activities (such as voting, contacting MPs, and holding an office in a political organisation). On this basis 7 per cent of the electorate are activists. Conduct a survey in your school or college to find out:

1 what proportion of students are 'very interested' in politics;
2 what proportion discuss politics 'frequently';
3 what proportion can be classified as 'activists'.

Government action to increase participation

The purported aim of a number of Government-led policies and reports has been to increase participation:

1 *The 1977 Bullock Report on Industrial Democracy*: this saw existing employee–employer relationships as failing 'to draw out people's energies and skills to anything like their full potential'. In order to involve people in decision-making at their place of work the Report proposed a '2X + Y' formula for companies with more than 2,000 employees. One group on the board of directors would consist of management representatives ('X'); one group on the

board would consist of trade union officers representing employees ('X'); and a smaller groups would consist of coopted independent directors recruited jointly by both sides ('Y'). The recommendations of the Bullock Report did not become law, but new proposals for introducing employee consultation are currently being considered by the European Union.

2 *The 1984 Trade Union Act*: this made it illegal for official strikes to take place without a secret ballot of the members involved. Members of union executive committees were required to stand for election at intervals of not more than five years, and unions had to hold ballots on retaining their political funds.

3 *The 1988 Employment Act*: this gave workers the right to sue their union if attempts were made to discipline them for failing to support industrial action. In 1999, the Blair Government intends to introduce 'Fairness at Work' legislation. This will give rights of recognition to trade unions and enable them to negotiate on behalf of their members.

4 *The 1988 Education Reform Act*: this gave parents the right to vote on whether their children's school should opt-out of local authority control and become grant maintained and funded by central government. (This policy was ended by the Blair Government.) Increased decision-making power was delegated to schools. A number of school governors were directly elected by parents. In 1998 new regulations were introduced which will enable parents to vote on the future of the country's 164 grammar schools. (Provided 20 per cent of eligible parents sign a petition a ballot will be held. In areas where more than 25 per cent of secondary places are selective, all parents of schoolchildren will be entitled to vote, but in other areas only parents in feeder schools will be entitled to vote.)

5 *The 1988 Housing Act*: this gave tenants the right to pick an approved landlord if they were not satisfied with their council as a landlord. Tenant Management Cooperatives could also be established. Between 1979 and 1997 1.6 million council houses were sold. Some supporters of this policy claimed that home ownership increases individuals' sense of autonomy. This could lead to greater political participation.

6 *The 1991 Citizen's Charter*: this was the Major administration's 'big idea'. John Major described it as being 'about giving more power to the citizen. It is a testament to our belief in people's right to be informed and to choose for themselves'. The Citizen's Charter included pledges to guarantee NHS patients maximum waiting times and ensure that schools and colleges published their examination results. (The idea of a Charter which would improve the efficiency of public services was first devised by the New York City Council in 1989.)

7 *The 1998 Report of the Advisory Group on Education for Citizenship and the Teaching of Democracy in Schools*: this declared that 'the teaching of citizenship and democracy is so important both for schools and the life of the nation that there should be a statutory requirement on schools that it is part of the

entitlement of all pupils'. It defined citizenship in terms of 'the knowledge, skills and values relevant to the nature and practices of participative democracy...'. The Report proposed that citizenship education should come into force by the year 2000 and would involve up to 5 per cent of curriculum time.

8 *The 1998 Jenkins Report*: this was a report on electoral reform in the UK. Supporters of electoral reform believe it will increase voter choice and thereby raise levels of political participation. In December 1997 the Government established a commission, led by Roy Jenkins, to investigate the best alternative 'system or combination of systems' to the existing first-past-the-post system of election to the House of Commons. In two of the last 15 elections the party which came second in votes won the most seats in Parliament (1951 and October 1974). Under the Jenkins proposals such a result could not recur. A close relationship would be established between the number of votes cast for a party and the number of seats it gained in Parliament. The report recommended that the first-past-the-post system be replaced with a new voting system in which electors have two-votes – one for the constituency MP and one for an additional or 'top-up' MP. The first vote ranks candidates in order of preference with any candidate getting 50 per cent of the vote being elected. (If no candidate polled 50 per cent, the least popular candidate is eliminated and his or her second preference votes are redistributed.) The second vote is used to ensure that the number of seats a party has in Parliament is broadly proportional to the number of votes it received in the election. Between 15 and 20 per cent of MPs would be elected as additional or 'top-up' members. The government has pledged that a new voting system will only be introduced after a referendum.

POINTS OF EVALUATION

1 The Bullock Report recommended that all of the workers' representatives on company boards should be trade union officers. Such a 'corporatist' approach means that employees who are not trade union officials or even members of trade unions would be excluded. Some companies have developed ways of involving employees in decision-making which do not fit with the '2X + Y' formula.

2 One aim of 1980s trade union reform was to weaken the power of trade unions and *reduce* forms of participation which involved industrial action (such as strikes, secondary picketing and workers' occupations of plants). Crouch describes the 1988 Employment Act as 'an extension of union democracy, though it is democracy of a guided kind, giving workers the right to do things that the government would like them to do' (in Dunleavy 1990).

3 Turn-outs in elections of parent-governors have been disappointing. Grant-maintained schools are no longer subject to control by elected councillors. Some grammar school heads have stated that they would opt for independent

(private) status rather than implement a democratic ballot which compelled them to become comprehensive.

4 Owner-occupation might improve an individual's sense of autonomy (unless mortgage arrears lead to the house being repossessed). Some Conservative Party strategists favoured extending owner-occupation for electoral reasons. It was seen as a method to weaken the Labour Party's political base in council estates since owner-occupiers were more likely to vote Conservative. In Hutton's view 'the fracturing of Britain into a 30:30:40 society is mirrored in the housing market: the affluent suburb; the rows of increasingly dilapidated semi-detached on the modern estates; and the ghettos of public housing' *Guardian*, 27.1.95. The reduction in the stock of council housing reduced the life-chances (and possibly the political participation) of the poorest groups in society.

5 The Citizen's Charter was based on a limited view of the citizen as a customer rather than as someone with wider political rights and obligations. The position of the apostrophe (Citizen's Charter rather than Citizens' Charter) reflects an individualistic perspective on politics: the citizen was viewed as a consumer rather than as a member of a collectivity. Most of the Charter pledges were vague and there was no provision for financial compensation if they were broken.

6 Citizenship education will form a small part of an already crowded school curriculum. The Advisory Group notes that 'the whole ethos of the school must be considered as relevant to the basis of active citizenship...'. Authoritarian schools may be reluctant to implement an effective programme of citizenship education.

7 All voting systems, not just the first-past-the post system, have weaknesses. The voting system proposed by the Jenkins Report would probably result in an increase in third party representation in Parliament. (In the 1997 General Election the Liberal Democrats would have gained 89 rather than 46 MPs.) The House of Common would become more representative of the spread of public opinion but the likelihood of one party gaining an overall majority would be reduced. Less stable coalition governments might be formed.

Activity

In small groups have a brainstorming session and formulate *two* policy proposals which could increase levels of political participation.

Revolution

As we have seen, political participation is not confined to activities which take place within the existing institutional framework. It can also take non-orthodox forms, and the most dramatic example of this is revolution. The term revolution is sometimes used to refer to major processes of social change. Gordon Childe located the urban revolution in 'the thousand years or so immediately preceding 3000 BC'. E. P. Thompson spoke of 'the bourgeois revolution of the fifteenth to the eighteenth century'.

Until the American Revolution of 1776 and the French Revolution of 1789 the term revolution signified a *return to the way things were*, a circular turning back to a previous state of affairs. In his study of the revolutionary decades of 1640–60 in England, Christopher Hill noted that 'whereas the trinities of the later revolutions – liberty, equality, fraternity; peace, bread and land – demanded something *new*, something to be fought for and achieved in the *future*, the trinity of the English revolutionaries – religion, liberty and property – was intended to defend what already existed, or was believed to exist' (1970).

Today, revolution refers to a mass movement which overthrows the established social order, takes control of State power, and initiates major political and social changes. Revolutions have been described as 'internal wars' since they involve the use (or the threat of use) of violence.

Theories of revolution

Theories explaining the outbreak of revolutions have focused on:

1. The existence of class contradictions and large-scale inequalities in wealth and power (the Marxist approach). In 1915, Lenin made the following note of revolutionary situations: 'the lower orders won't, the upper classes can't, growth of misery, extraordinary activity'.
2. The existence of strains and tensions which produce a state of disequilibrium in society (the functionalist approach). In the view of Chalmers Johnson, revolutions 'need not occur at all' – provided governments respond to political crises in a creative and intelligent way and avoid 'dysfunctional' actions. He notes that war has often been a catalyst for revolution (eg the Russia and Chinese revolutions).
3. Crane Brinton studied the English, American, French and Russian Revolutions (the historical approach). He found there were a number of 'tentative uniformities' in all four societies: they were improving economically before the revolution took place; bitter class antagonisms existed; intellectuals transferred their allegiance to the revolutionaries; the government machinery was inefficient; the old governing class was politically inept.
4. Charles Tilly argues that 'in the modern European experience repressive forces are themselves the most consistent initiators and performers of collective violence' (the conflict management approach). Governments have

reacted to mass protests and demonstrations with coercion and brutal violence, and this has provoked the very revolution that the authorities intended to repress.

5 Alexis de Tocqueville observed that 'it is not always by going from bad to worse that a country falls into revolution. It happens most frequently that a people, which had supported the most crushing laws without complaint, and apparently as if they were unfelt, throws them off with violence as soon as the burden begins to be diminished' (the relative deprivation and rising expectations approach). James Davies also argues that the likelihood of revolution increases when living conditions have been *improving*, when there is 'an intolerable gap between what people want and what they get'.

Activity

In 1997 the international financier George Soros declared that 'we are not anywhere near a revolution, except perhaps in France'. In small groups list five key factors which would suggest that a potentially revolutionary situation existed in a society.

VOTING BEHAVIOUR

The study of voting behaviour is known as **psephology**. The ancient Athenians used pebbles (psepholos) to vote in elections.

THE 1997 GENERAL ELECTION

The following are important features of this election:

- The Labour Party gained 13,518,167 votes (43.2 per cent of the vote) and 418 Labour MPs were elected – the largest number ever and an increase of 146 compared with 1992. The swing from Conservative to Labour was 10 per cent – the greatest since 1945. The 179 seat majority was the largest since 1935.
- The Conservative Party gained 9,600,943 votes (30.7 per cent of the vote). 165 Conservative MPs were elected, a decrease of 178 compared with 1992. The share of the vote was the lowest since 1832, and the number of candidates elected was the lowest since 1906.
- The Liberal Democrats gained 5,242,947 votes (17.2 per cent of the vote) and 46 Liberal Democrat MPs were elected – more than double the number (20) elected in 1992.
- Plaid Cymru (the Welsh Nationalists) gained 10 per cent of the Welsh vote and four MPs. The SNP (the Scottish Nationalists) gaines 22.5 per cent of the

Scottish vote and six MPs. The Conservative Party gained 19 per cent of the vote in Wales and 17.5 per cent of the vote in Scotland, but did not win a single seat in either Scotland or Wales. Sinn Fein gained 16.1 per cent of the vote in Northern Ireland (an increase of 6 per cent on 1992) and two MPs.

- The Referendum Party (financed by the late Sir James Goldsmith) had 547 candidates, gained 811,827 votes (2.6 per cent of the vote), but did not win any seats.
- The total number of votes cast was 31,286,284 and a total of 659 MPs were elected.
- Election turn-out was 71.2 per cent the lowest since 1935. This was, however, still significantly higher than election turn-outs in the USA: in the Congressional elections of 1998 only 37 per cent of registered voters actually voted.
- The electoral system worked to the disadvantage of the Conservative Party. It gained over 31 per cent of the votes but only 25 per cent of the seats in Parliament. The Labour Party's share of the vote was lower than it achieved at any election between 1945 and 1966. Of those eligible to vote only three in 10 voted for the Labour Party.
- 120 women MPs were elected and 259 new MPs won seats – this was more than in any postwar election.
- 32 per cent of women voted Conservative, 44 per cent voted Labour, and 17 per cent voted Liberal Democrat.
- 31 per cent of men voted Conservative, 44 per cent voted Labour, and 17 per cent voted Liberal Democrat.
- 42 per cent of AB (professional/managerial) voters supported the Conservative Party, 31 per cent supported the Labour Party, and 21 per cent supported the Liberal Democrats.
- 61 per cent of DE (semi-skilled and unskilled manual) voters supported the Labour Party, 21 per cent supported the Conservative Party, and 13 per cent supported the Liberal Democrats.
- 41 per cent of home owners voted Labour, while 35 per cent voted Conservative.
- 65 per cent of council tenants voted Labour, while 13 per cent voted Conservative.
- 57 per cent of trade union members voted Labour, while 18 per cent voted Conservative.
- 57 per cent of first time voters supported Labour, 19 per cent supported the Conservatives, and 18 per cent supported the Liberal Democrats.
- 44 per cent of those aged 65 and over supported the Conservatives, 34 per cent supported Labour, and 16 per cent supported the Liberal Democrats.

Study point

The data given above on votes cast for parties is taken from definitive publications. However a check of the main sources (books, articles, and newspapers) will reveal slight differences in the number of votes parties are said to have received. All statistics are problematic – even objective psephological ones. Think of reasons why these discrepancies may arise.

Press Coverage

Scammell and Harrop point out that the 1997 General Election 'was a landmark in the political history of Britain's press. It was the first campaign in which Labour secured the support of most national daily newspapers. Six of the 10 backed Labour: the *Sun*, the *Daily Star*, the *Financial Times* just about, the *Guardian*, the *Independent* and the *Mirror*, the last three combining their preference for Labour with an appeal for anti-Conservative tactical voting. Conservative support was confined to the *Express*, the *Daily Mail* and the *Daily Telegraph*, with *The Times* advocating a vote for Euro-sceptic candidates of varied hue' (in Butler and Kavanagh, 1997). Papers which supported the Labour Party had 21.6 million readers and papers which supported the Conservative Party had 10.6 million readers.

Study point

Here is a list of postwar British Prime Ministers. Which political party did they represent?

- Attlee 1945–51
- Churchill 1951–5
- Eden 1955–7
- Macmillan 1957–63
- Douglas-Home 1963–4
- Wilson 1964–70
- Heath 1970–4
- Wilson 1974–6
- Callaghan 1976–9
- Thatcher 1979–90
- Major 1990–7
- Blair 1997–

Answers on page 136.

REFERENDUMS

In a referendum a specific question is referred to the electorate. Referendums have been held in the UK on the following questions:

- Sunday opening of licensed premises in Wales. These can be held every seven years and are triggered by 500 local electors in a district signing a petition. Turn-outs have varied from 8.7 per cent to 57 per cent.
- Whether Northern Ireland should remain part of the UK. In March 1973 98.9 per cent voted 'yes' and 1.1 per cent voted 'no'. The referendum was boycotted by the Nationalist population. Turnout was 58.1 per cent.
- Whether the UK should stay in the European Community. In June 1975 67.2 per cent voted 'yes' and 32.8 per cent voted 'no'. Turnout was 63.2 per cent.
- Whether a devolved assembly should be established in Scotland and the Scotland Act 1978 be approved. In March 1979 51.5 per cent voted 'yes' and 48.3 per cent voted 'no'. Turnout was 62.9 per cent. For devolution to proceed the support of 40 per cent of the electorate (ie those eligible to vote) was required. Only 32.5 per cent of the *electorate* voted in favour.
- Whether a devolved assembly should be established in Wales and the Wales Act 1978 be approved. In March 1979 20.3 per cent voted 'yes' and 79.7 per cent voted 'no'. Turnout was 58.3 per cent.
- Whether a Scottish Parliament should be established. In September 1997, 74.3 per cent voted 'yes' and 25.7 per cent voted 'no'. On whether a Scottish Parliament should be given limited tax varying powers 63.5 per cent voted 'yes' and 36.5 per cent voted 'no'. Turnout was 60.4 per cent.
- Whether a Welsh Assembly should be established. In September 1997, 50.3 per cent voted 'yes' and 49.7 per cent voted 'no'. Turn-out was 50 per cent.
- Whether London should have an elected Mayor. In May 1998, 72 per cent voted 'yes' and 28 per cent voted 'no'. Turn-out was 34 per cent.
- Whether the Good Friday Agreement on the future of Northern Ireland should be supported. In May 1998, 71.12 per cent voted 'yes' and 28.88 per cent voted 'no'. Turn-out was 81 per cent.

Support for referendums

Those who support the use of referendums argue:

1. They provide an opportunity for citizens to engage in political decision-making.
2. They increase political education.
3. They are useful when political parties have failed to develop a clear position on a specific issue.
4. They ensure that policies have the consent of the governed.
5. In general elections, voters may vote for a party even though they are opposed to a specific policy contained in its manifesto. Referendums enable voters to express their view on a particular issue. General elections are 'blunt instruments'.
6. Referendums and **initiatives** enable citizens to participate in direct democracy. They have been widely used in the USA, Austria, Italy, and Switzerland. (Initiatives are proposals for changes in the law which come from the electorate rather than from the government. A minimum number of electors trigger the initiative proposal, which then has to win majority support.)

Opposition to referendums

Those who oppose the use of referendums argue that:

1 They undermine the principle of parliamentary sovereignty: key policies should be decided by elected representatives.
2 They can be manipulated by the government: the question put to the people can be phrased in a way which favours a particular response.
3 They undermine the principle of representative government: issues need to be debated in depth in the legislature.
4 They undermine the principle of responsible government: the government has to lead public opinion and not simply follow it.
5 A closely contested referendum could be decided by the side which has the most money and is able to buy the most effective advertising.

Activity

The Blair government has stated that it will hold referendums on electoral reform and on joining the single European currency. In small groups debate whether more frequent use of referendums will enhance or undermine parliamentary democracy.

BY-ELECTIONS

By elections are held when a sitting MP in a constituency dies or retires. There is a high level of media coverage and parties usually invest considerable resources in the campaign. Tactical voting increases and there is often a strong protest vote against the governing party. Turn-outs in by-elections are lower than in general elections, and any successes by minority parties are usually reversed when a general election is held.

KEY FACTORS INFLUENCING VOTING BEHAVIOUR

- *Social class*: the Labour Party has been most successful in winning the support of semi- and unskilled manual workers. The Conservative Party has been most successful in winning the support of the middle-class (especially small business owners). A key category is the C2s (skilled manual workers). In 1997 the Labour Party gained 54 per cent of the C2 vote.
- *Gender*: in most postwar elections women have been more likely to vote Conservative than men. But in the 1997 General Election the gender gap disappeared.
- *Age*: the young are more likely to support the Labour Party, while those who are retired are more likely to support the Conservative Party. In 1997 more

than two-fifths of those aged 65 or over supported the Conservative Party compared with a fifth of voters in the 18–29 age groups.

- *Ethnicity*: members of the Afro-Caribbean community (and to a lesser extent members of the Asian community) are far more likely to vote Labour than Conservative. Around 80 per cent of 'ethnic minority voters' support the Labour Party. 'Ethnic minorities' represent over 15 per cent of the electorate in 56 constituencies and could have a key influence in a closely contested election.

Study point

'Ethnic minorities' tends to be used as a shorthand term to refer to members of the Afro-Caribbean and Asian communities. But it is a problematic concept. In your view, can members of other culturally distinctive groups (eg the Jewish community, and Irish people living in Britain) be referred to as 'ethnic minorities'?

- *Region and locality*: the Conservative Party is more successful in the South and the Labour Party is more successful in the North. (To a lesser extent the Conservative Party is more successful in the East and the Labour Party is more successful in the West.) In the 1997 General Election the Conservative Party failed to win a single seat in Wales or Scotland. The political culture of neighbourhood and locality has a significant influence on voting patterns (eg middle-class people in Glasgow are more likely to vote Labour than middle-class people in Bath).

Study point

1 What are the key factors which influence the way *you* vote?
2 List some ideological differences between political parties.

THEORIES OF VOTING BEHAVIOUR

Deviant Voters: Working-Class Conservatives and Middle-Class Radicals

In general elections at least a third of manual workers 'deviate' from their class and vote for the Conservative Party. One explanation of working-class Conservative support has been in terms of **deference** – a strong preference and exaggerated respect for political leaders who have high social status.

Ralph Samuel found that a third of the working-class voters he interviewed in Stevenage New Town were deferential. Respondents told him: 'The Conservative

Party is the gentleman's party. They're the people who have the money. I always vote for them.' 'You need brains and money to run the country in an efficient way, and working-class people can't have that. The Conservatives are better suited to running the country. They are better educated – I think there is nothing better than to hear a Public School man speak English...' (1960).

McKenzie and **Silver** studied 604 working-class voters in six constituencies. A distinction was drawn between Deferentials (who believed that Conservative leaders were 'Born to Rule') and Seculars (who supported the Conservative Party on the basis of a pragmatic assessment of its policies and performance): 26 per cent of the sample were found to be deferential. The book's title – *Angels in Marble* – was taken from an 1883 editorial in The *Times*: 'In the inarticulate mass of the English populace, Disraeli discerned the Conservative working man as the sculptor perceives the angel prisoned in a block of marble' (1968).

Parkin turned the debate about working-class Conservatives upside down and described workers who voted for the Labour Party as the 'deviant' voters. The dominant value system is shaped by 'establishment' institutions such as the monarchy, the aristocracy, the public schools, and Oxford and Cambridge universities. Voting for the Labour Party is a 'symbolic act of deviance' – a rejection of the status quo. Such deviant voting will only be widespread where it is buttressed by a strong collectivist counter-culture (eg working-class areas in the North, Wales, and Scotland where there is a trade union and labour movement tradition). The absence of an 'alternative normative sub-system' in middle-class areas (such as spa towns and seaside resorts) means that a high proportion of manual workers conform to the dominant values and vote Conservative (1967).

Parkin also studied 'deviant' members of the middle-class who support the Labour Party. A survey of Campaign for Nuclear Disarmament (CND) marchers in 1965 found that middle-class Labour voters were drawn mainly from the 'educated stratum'. Their occupations, for example as public sector social workers and teachers, served as 'sanctuaries for middle-class radicalism' (1968).

Political Socialisation and Party Identification

The Labour Party was not founded until 1900 and it was only in the 1920s that it became a major national party. Before 1919 six out of seven constituencies had never had a Labour candidate.

Butler and **Stokes** focus on the influence of political socialisation (1974). In 1963 they interviewed 2009 electors in 80 constituencies in the UK. They found that parents had a major influence on the political thinking of their children.

'A child is very likely to share the parent's party preference. Partisanship over the individual's lifetime has some of the quality of a photographic reproduction that deteriorates with time: it is a fairly sharp copy of the parent's original at the beginning of political awareness, but over the years it becomes somewhat blurred, although easily recognisable.'

In 1963, 75 per cent of voters who 'identified' with the Conservative Party came from homes where both parents were Conservatives, and 81 per cent of voters who 'identified' with the Labour Party came from homes where both parents were Labour supporters. (The **expressive** interpretation of voting sees it as an expression of an individual's social background and loyalties.) Even if voters disagree with a party's policies they may still continue to vote for it. Only a minority are 'floaters' who switch their support from one party to another. Most have enduring loyalties to the party they first identified with.

In the 1950s and 1960s the parents of many individuals from working-class backgrounds had not been socialised into supporting the Labour Party. Their parents had grown up in an era when politics was dominated by the Liberal Party and the Conservative Party. The study predicted that support for the Labour Party would grow since a new generation of voters would have undergone political socialisation in Labour-voting homes.

Curtice sums up Butler and Stokes' theory as follows:

> 'Football fans do not decide who to go and watch on the basis of which team has the best tactics. Rather, they watch their 'own' team, even if they are at the bottom of the league. Butler and Stokes suggested voters form just the same emotional attachments to a political party ... Where does football partisanship come from? Passed on from generation to generation as father introduces son to to the terraces. So equally, Butler and Stokes argued, political partisanship is passed from mother to daughter as they talk in the home' Times Higher Education Supplement, 18.11.94

Study point

Conduct a survey to find out how many individuals in your class support the same political party as their parents.

Rational Choice Theory or Issue Voting

Voting is analysed in **instrumental** terms. The 'rational' individual carefully weighs up the costs and benefits to be gained from supporting a particular political party. Maximisation of economic self-interest is the name of the game. According to **Anthony Downs** (1957) voters assess the 'utility income' they have received from the existing government, in terms of the quality of their children's State education, standards of NHS health care, crime rates, tax levels and so on. They work out if their 'utility income' would have been greater if the opposition party has been in government, and then decide to vote for the party which seems most likely to 'deliver the goods' and maximise benefits for themselves and their families. The party which is judges as offering the greatest net benefits to voters wins. In the 1997 General Election the five most important (or 'salient') issues for the electorate were health care, education, law and order, unemployment and pensions. On each of these issues the Labour Party has a clear lead in opinion polls over the Conservative Party.

Hilde Himmelweit also studied voting in terms of individuals who 'rationally' seek to maximise their individual self-interest. Her 'consumer model of vote choice' was based on a small longitudinal sample of male voters in London from the time they cast their first vote in 1959 through to their sixth vote in October 1974. Voters were viewed as informed consumers who support the party which offers the best match with their own policy preference. 'We compared the way the voter decides how to vote with how he decides what goods to buy. Instead of buying goods, the individual purchases a party...' In a situation where 'all the parties are found wanting but they still wish to vote' voters will seek 'a *minimal-regret* solution, and vote for the party which offends their views least'. Himmelweit's analysis of voting (like Downs) is based on the idea of the 'rationally' of the voter – it assumes that 'the voter wished to maximise his or her expected utilities'. There is no place in this model for the 'voting masochist' who sets out 'to select a party which would make matters worse' (1981).

Harrop and Miller summarise Himmelweit's analysis as follows: 'most citizens treat elections like a shopping expedition; they are on the look-out for fresh ideas and new parties as well as old favourites. Although the voters' information may be skimpy or even wrong electors are at least making a conscious, individual and instrumental choice: *voters decide*!' (1987).

Embourgeoisement and new social trends

The Labour Party lost three General Elections in a row in 1951, 1955, and 1959. In 1961 **Ferdinand Zweig** put forward the embourgeoisement thesis and claimed that affluence and prosperity were eroding working-class support for the Labour Party. Workers were discarding their cloth caps and acquiring middle-class life styles complete with washing machines, package holidays, mortgages – and votes for the Conservative Party.

The Labour Party also experienced four successive defeats in the General Elections of 1979, 1983, 1987, and 1992. **Ivor Crewe** formulated a revised version of the embourgeoisement thesis and claimed that 'the embourgeoisement of British society has undoubtedly tilted the balance of partisanship in the Conservatives' favour'. A new working-class was said to have emerged (Southern, skilled, home-owning) which had an instrumental outlook on politics. Its votes would go to the party which seemed most likely to deliver a high standard of living.

> The rapid spread of home-ownership, the migration from North to South and from inner-city to suburb, and the expansion of non-union private sector employment have undermined working-class loyalty to the Labour Party.' 'Social and cultural change is slowly eroding its normal vote. Demographic trends for the 1990s – embourgeoisement, de-unionisation, migration, ageing – are not on its side' (1993).

Even amongst manual workers who continued to vote Labour, support for the Party's 'collectivist trinity' (public ownership, the welfare state, and trade unions) was on the wane. There was a widening ideological gap between party activists and Labour's 'natural' supporters.

The view that sociological trends were making it increasingly difficult for the Labour Party to win elections was summarised by Martin Linton as follows:

> 'Every Labour stronghold is losing population, the inner cities, the North, the Clyde, the mining industry, the heavy engineering industries, the public sector, the trade unions, whereas every Conservative stronghold is growing, the South, the rural areas, the service sector, the City ... the problem for Labour stems from its failure to project a "popular socialism" that appeals to the better paid, skilled, southern, home-owning working classes' (1988).

Sectoral Cleavages or the radical voting model

Some individuals are employed in the public sector (eg a teacher in a comprehensive school) while others are employed in the private sector (eg a car worker in the Ford Motor Company): this is the **production sector effect**. Some individuals rely on the public sector for services (they live in a council house and use the National Health Service) while others rely on the private sector for services (they own their own house and have private medical insurance): this is the **consumption sector effect**. Some individuals are supported by the State (pensioners and the unemployed): this is known as the **state dependence effect**.

- According to **Dunleavy** and **Husbands** these divisions (or **cleavages**) constitute a new political fault line in society which cuts through traditional linkages between class and party (1985).
- A higher proportion of those employed in the public sector are members of trade unions than private sector workers. They are likely to have different interests and favour different government policies, for example to be more sympathetic to 'tax and spend' policies.
- If the consumption sector effect is combined with the production sector effect, the impact on voting behaviour could be significant. A public sector council worker and council tenant will have a clear interest in voting Labour, while a private sector worker who owns his or her own house will not. Sectoral cleavages cut through traditional class divisions.

Class Dealignment Theory

The period from 1950–70 has been described as the 'Era of Alignment'. (1950 was the first 'normal' postwar election since nearly 3 million electors were registered as service voters in 1945). Class was aligned with voting. Almost two-thirds of manual workers voted Labour and over two-thirds of the middle-class voted Conservative. The two party system was dominant (around 90 per cent of votes was cast for either the Labour or Conservative Party) and there was a high level of **partisan alignment**: many voters identified with and felt a strong sense of loyalty towards a particular political party.

The period from 1970 until the present day has been described as the 'Era of Dealignment.' Electoral volatility has increased: more voters have switched their voting preferences from one election to another. Tactical voting – supporting a party which is not the first choice in order to prevent a least-liked party being elected – has become more common. While short-term political factors, such as divisions within the Labour Party, contributed to the Conservative Party's electoral success, long-term social trends were working in its favour.

There has been a shift from a two-party towards a multi-party system. Fewer than 80 per cent of votes are now cast for the two main parties; support has grown for the Liberal Democrats and Nationalist parties; voters are less likely to strongly identify with a particular party. Underpinning these changes is **class dealignment** – the weakening of the relationship between class and political allegiance.

Denver (1989) points out that in 1987 only 16 per cent of voters were 'very strong identifiers' with the Conservative or Labour Party. This compares with an average of 40 per cent during the period 1964–70. With more extensive television coverage of politics and increased education, the electorate has become more informed and politically sophisticated. Neither of the major parties was 'a dazzling success' when in government and this experience further weakened party loyalities. By the early 1980s rising levels of prosperity has led to half of manual workers being owner-occupiers (compared with a fifth in the mid-1950s). A growing proportion of households were 'mixed-class', that is one partner in a manual and the other in a non-manual job. Manual workers were – for the fist time – a minority of the labour force, and the class structure was fragmenting. The links between voting behaviour and social class were far weaker in the 'Era of Dealignment' than they had been in the 'Era of Alignment'.

Interactionist Interpretation

Voting behaviour is shaped by the interaction between social structure and politics. Voting choices are influenced by both the social location of individuals *and* their perception of the performance of political parties. Both less expressive factors (the political loyalities acquired during childhood) *and* instrumental factors (calculations of benefits which will result from particular government policies) are at work.

Heath, **Jowell** and **Curtis** (1985) argue that electoral choices are not soley inherited from childhood socialisation. A party with a credible leadership, an image of unity, and convincing policies will win new support. 'A party's ideological stance will affect the level of support it can command.' Instead of subscribing to 'a naive "sociological determinism"' psephology must recognise that 'public attitudes can be shaped by political leadership as well as by social change.' Instrumental explanations of voting fail since one vote would make no difference to a result and consequently a 'rational, instrumental voter would never waste his time going to the ballot box'. An 'expressive or moral element' has to be introduced 'to explain the act of voting itself'.

Heath et al also reject the class dealignment thesis: 'there is no direct evidence that the classes have weakened in cohesion.' The sharp fall in the number of votes cast for the Labour Party between 1964 and 1983 (by some 3.8 million) can be explained in terms of the decline in the size of the manual working-class and the poor political performance of the Labour Party itself. It was not the result of a weakening of class loyalties: an 'Era of Alignment' was *not* being followed by an 'Era of Dealignment'. The relative strength of support for political parties in different classes stayed much the same. Members of the petty bourgeoisie (small proprietors, farmers and own-account manual workers) continued to vote overwhelmingly for the Conservative Party. Support for the Labour Party continued to be concentrated amongst rank-and-file manual workers. Class differences, 'whether with respect to objective inequalities, subjective values or support for the political parties, remained at much the same level throughout the postwar period. Whether for better or worse, Britain is still divided by class'.

Study point

On a postcard complete a table to summarise the details of theories of voting behaviour.

Theories of voting behaviour		
KEY THEORY	KEY AUTHOR	KEY ARGUMENTS

POINTS OF EVALUATION

1 Deference only provides *partial* explanation for working-class support for the Conservative Party.

- A study of 320 male working-class Conservative voters by Nordlinger found that only 28 per cent (compared with 26 per cent of the *Angels in Marble* sample) could be classified as deferential voters (1967).

- Deference has been a declining force in British political culture. In Kavanagh's view the concept of the deferential English 'attained the status of a stereotype' and lacks empirical credibility (1971).
- Working-class Conservatives have often been portrayed as 'deviants'. But Birch argues that there are simply too many of them 'for it to be reasonable to regard them as deviants' (1998). In 1951 some 6.2 million manual workers voted Conservative.

2 Political socialisation is only one of a number of factors which influence voting behaviour. The performance of parties in office, the quality of party leadership and the popular appeal of party policies all have an important influence.

- In 1974 Butler and Stokes predicted that electoral demography would increasingly favour the Labour Party. Yet just nine years later (in the 1983 General Election) Labour's vote had fallen by 3 million and its share of the vote was only 2.2 per cent ahead of the Liberal/SDP Alliance.
- Rose and McAllister see childhood socialisation as simply 'the first of a series of steps by which an individual learns party loyalities'. Others include socio-economic interests; occupation; trade union membership; home-ownership; political values (eg ideas about government spending on social programmes); spatial context (the area and region in which an individual lives); and the current performance of parties (if a party 'fails to deliver the goods then people may reject it on the grounds of inadequate performance'). The loyalties that individuals express in voting 'are formed from a lifetime of experiences' (1990).

3 If voters were only motivated by the pursuit of 'rational' self-interest there would be little point in spending time and energy by going to vote at all. An individual seeking to increase his or her 'utility income' would do something else – bargain hunting in shops or putting in overtime at work.

- It is misleading to compare a voter to a consumer. Voting decisions are influenced by an individual's political socialisation and pre-existing party loyalities. The same does not apply to the decisions made by a shopper on what to purchase.

4 The embourgeoisement thesis is a form of 'sociological determinism' – it ignores the autonomy and fluidity of politics. Changes in the social structure and in material living standards are not automatically translated into changes in voting preferences.

- Political parties can change their image and appeal to new voters. In 1964 Wilson's Labour Party discarded the cloth-cap image and 're-branded' itself as a modernising technocratic party. In 1997 Tony Blair 're-branded' the Labour Party as 'New Labour' and won new support from the middle-class and skilled workers in the Midlands and the South.
- The classic study of the *Affluent Worker in the Class Structure* (1969) by Goldthorpe et al made the point that improvements in manual workers' material living standards do not mean they suddenly start seeing themselves as middle-class.

A washing machine is a washing machine, not a sociological gadget which miraculously transforms its owners' blue collar status into white collar status.

- The correlation between a period of rising living standards for four-fifths of the population and the Labour Party losing elections (in 1970, 1983, 1987, 1992) is not the same as causation. The latter may not have been *caused* the former.

5 The division between private sector and public sector interests is not a clear cut one. Many voters depend on *both* sectors, for example a private sector worker with an NHS doctor whose children attend state schools and a public sector worker with private medical insurance who is an owner-occupier.

- Users of private education and private health care have always been overwhelmingly Conservative voters, while those dependent on public sector council housing have always been predominantly Labour voters. Sectoral cleavages do not represent a new division in British politics.
- The success of the Labour Party in the 1997 General Election undermines the claim that sectoral cleavages constitute a major political fault line. It gained support from both sides of the sectoral divide (including the votes of a majority of owner-occupiers).

6 In the view of Heath et al, the class dealignment thesis is basically flawed: class continues to exert a strong influence on voting.

- Detailed occupational analysis indicates that the proportion of *ordinary* manual workers who support the Labour Party has not changed significantly. It was workers who exercised some authority (eg self-employed manual workers and manual workers with supervisory positions) who were most likely to vote Conservative during the Thatcher–Major years.
- During the years of Conservative Party dominance in the 1980s, the Labour Party continued to win more support than other parties from 'rank-and-file' manual workers. Rather than having a 'classless' appeal the Liberal/SDP Alliance was most popular amongst the new middle-class employed in the public sector. Core support for the Conservative Party continued to be concentrated amongst the self-employed, and managers and professionals in the private sector.
- The fragmentation of the working-class into different strata is nothing new. Marshall et al note that 'sectionalism, privatism and instrumentalism have always been close to the surface of working-class life' (1988).

7 Since 1950 significant changes have taken place in both the social structure and the landscape of politics. The relationship between class and voting has not stayed constant.

- Only by radically redefining the working-class and dramatically shrinking its size to a rank-and-file 'core' can Heath et al put forward the claim that class dealignment has not taken place.
- There is no doubt that partisan dealignment has increased. A 1964 survey found that only 12 per cent said their party identification was *not* strong – by

1992 this had increased to 35 per cent. The process of partisan dealignment is closely linked to class dealignment.

- The growth in support for third parties provides further evidence of the weakening of the links between class and voting. In 1997 the share of the vote gained by the Liberal Democrats was more than six times greater than that gained by the Liberal Party in 1951. If class was *the* key to voting, individuals would vote for 'their' class party – not for 'non-class' parties like the Liberal Democrats and the Welsh and Scottish Nationalists.
- The emergence of a more fragmented class structure and the increased influence of the mass media has 'dealigned' traditional patterns of voting. One of the rationales of the 'New Labour' project is to respond to the declining force of class in British society and to take 'class' out of the Labour Party's ideological mind-set. In a speech to the Labour Party Conference in October 1996 Tony Blair declared: 'Forget the past. No more bosses and workers. We are on the same side.'

Study point

Information on election results and access to a wide range of political resources is available on the London School of Economics website:

http://www.lse.ac.uk
Scroll down and click on 'Hotlist'.

SUMMARY

- Political participation varies with class, gender, life-cycle stage, ethnicity, residential location, socialisation experiences and personality factors.
- There has been a downward trend in membership of political parties, and an upward trend in membership of pressure groups.
- A quarter of the population takes no part in political activity.
- Government-led proposals to increase participation have focused on industrial democracy, trade unions, schools, housing policy, the Citizen's Charter, and citizenship education.
- Theories explaining the causes of revolutions have focused on class conflict, dysfunctional strains and tensions, historical uniformities, conflict management strategies, relative deprivation and rising expectations.
- Factors influencing voting behaviour include social class, family background, gender (although not in the 1997 General Election), age, ethnicity, region and locality, and the political performance and credibility of parties.
- Explanations of voting behaviour have focused on 'deviant' voting, political socialisation, rational choice, embourgeoisement and new social trends, sectoral cleavages, class dealignment, and interactionist theory.

Group work

Conduct a survey of levels of political literacy amongst the General Public. Interview individuals of different gender, age, and social backgrounds. Questions could include:

- What is the name of your local MP?
- Which political party does he or she represent?
- What is the name of your MEP?
- Which political party does he or she represent?
- What is the name of one of your local councillors?
- Name three government ministers.

A survey conducted by students in Lincoln found that 58 per cent of the public were able to name the local MP, 30 per cent were able to name the MEP, 42 per cent could name a local councillor, and 48 per cent could name three government ministers.

Practice Questions

1. 'An Era of Alignment in voting behaviour in Britain has been succeeded by an Era of Dealignment.' Explain and discuss.
2. Critically examine the view that voters – like consumers – are essentially rational instrumentalists who are motivated by economic self-interest.
3. 'Levels of political participation are directly related to the economic, social, and cultural resources individuals have at their disposal.' Discuss.

Coursework suggestions

1. Conduct a study of levels of political participation in your local area. Primary data could be based on a survey of a random sample of the public. (How many respondents are members of political parties and/or pressure groups, attend political meetings, have been in contact with MPs, MEPs and councillors, have distributed leaflets and/or canvassed for parties during election campaigns, have joined demonstrations, participated in protest actions?) Make use of secondary data such as turn-out rates in elections.
2. Examine the relationship between social class and voting behaviour. Interview individuals of different ages, gender, and class backgrounds. Establish their voting intentions for the future and their voting patterns in the past. Relate your empirical findings to the theoretical debate on class dealignment.

7

GLOBALISATION AND THE NEW POLITICS

Introduction

THIS CHAPTER EXAMINES the nature of globalisation; its impact on the state and political agency; the emergence of new social problems in a risk society; and signs of transition towards 'New Times'. Shifts towards a more fragmented and individualistic society, and the creation of a media-saturated culture, are changing political consciousness. The class-based ideologies associated with the 'Old Politics' have been in decline. Today's political agenda now includes post-materialist issues of identity, culture and ecology as well as issues of economic management, inequality and social exclusion. Powerful global forces, the decline of tradition, awareness of human rights, and the growth in individual reflexivity are ushering in an era of 'New Politics'.

DEFINING GLOBALISATION

Mass transportation and new forms of communication have compressed time and space and 'shrunk' the world. Every day a trillion US dollars' worth of speculative currency is transferred across State frontiers. Commodities are brought into our homes by a complex transnational system of economic exchange. An explosion in the Ukraine causes life-threatening damage to the ecology of North Wales. An Iranian plane is shot down over the Gulf of Arabia and a group responds by blowing up a plane in Europe. An economic crisis erupts in South-East Asia and workers at factories in the North-East of England are handed redundancy notices.

shared cultural experience. Electronically transmitted information enables geographically distant units to be organisationally unified. Companies operate on a world scale, moving in and out of countries in order to take advantage of low wages, low taxes, and low strike rates. '... the fast-frozen relations of organised capitalism which were structured around class, city, region, nation, the party, and even the world – are melting into the air' ('The End of Organised Capitalism' in Hall and Jacques, 1989).

Study point

Tabulate, on a postcard, the authors listed in this section. Make brief summary points of the key parts of their definitions.

AUTHOR	KEY CONCEPTS	KEY POINTS

THE IMPACT OF GLOBALISATION ON POLITICS

The Power of the State is weakened

- *Economic impact*: capital is highly mobile and can be rapidly transferred from one country to another. Key sectors of economic activity are removed from State control: the global market rules. In the past the movement of investment and currency was closely regulated and the State possessed considerable power over economic life. Today – in the words of Subcomandante Marcos in the Chiapas region of Mexico – 'In the cabaret of globalisation, the state goes through a striptease and by the end of its performance is left with the bare necessities only: its powers of repression ... the nation-state becomes a simple security service for the mega-companies ...' (Quoted in Bauman, 1998).
- *Political impact*: The decline in the economic power of the State has been followed by a decline in its political power. Lash and Urry (1994) describe the nation-state as 'being "hollowed out"... Its powers are being delegated upwards to supraregional or international bodies, downwards to regional or local states or to the private sector, inwards to relatively autonomous cross-national alliances. Such a hollowed-out state has its powers weakened at the same time that its legitimacy is challenged.
- *Social impact*: In the view of the French theorist **Alain Minc** a 'New Middle Ages' is returning: the authority of the centralised State is being weakened and endemic conflicts and semi-civil wars will break out between different groups in society. **John Gray** refers to contemporary Russian society as 'anarcho-capitalism'.

Political control over economic forces is weakened

Deregulation and computerisation of the world's financial markets enables enormous sums of capital to be speedily switched from one country to another. In Bauman's view the result is that 'no one seems now to be in control'. Political agency – the capacity to impose political control over events by deciding on a course of action and then carrying it through – is eroded. International markets, not governments, determine stock market prices, interest rates and exchange rates. 'The deepest meaning conveyed by the idea of globalisation is that of the indeterminate, unruly and self-propelled character of world affairs; the absence of a centre, of a controlling desk, of a board of directors, of a managerial office' (1998).

New social problems emerge

Because the State is 'less able to provide effective central control of economic life' (Giddens, 1994) the welfare state declines and inequality increases. Corporations switch their investments from high tax to low tax countries and the revenue needed to fund health, education and benefits falls. **Edward Soja** (1989) has charted the impact of 'transnational or global capital' on the social geography of modern life. 'Regional wars for jobs' take place as rival government agencies compete against each other for new investment by offering grants and incentive packages. Increased mobility of capital and labour reshapes the texture of city life.

> 'Perhaps as many as 250,000 people in Los Angeles County are living in transformed garages and backyard buildings, with half as many crowded into motel and hotel rooms hoping to save enough to pay the required deposits on more stable but out of reach rental accommodations. Many are forced to "hotbed", taking turns sleeping on never-empty mattresses, while others find accommodation in cinemas which obligingly reduce their charges after midnight. Those even less fortunate live on the streets and under the freeways, in cardboard boxes and makeshift tents, pooling together to form the largest homeless population in the United States – another "first" for Los Angeles.'

New forms of inequality and exclusion are created. Members of 'the increasingly cosmopolitan, extraterritorial world of global businessmen, global culture managers or global academics find that State borders are levelled down' (Bauman). But others – especially the poor of the economically less-developed Third World – find that immigration controls are tightened and borders built up. Lasch (1995) has spoken of the 'revolt of the elites'. While the poor are trapped in decaying cities the wealthy withdraw into fortress retreats and cease to participate in public institutions.

The politics of risk assume a new significance

Conflicts over the distribution of 'goods' – income, jobs, social security – are central to politics. With globalisation conflicts over 'bads' – the risks and costs associated with high technology – add a new dimension to political life. Human beings have always faced risks such as famines and floods. But many of the risks people face today are manufactured risks – risks which have been created by human-made scientific 'progress'. **Ulrich Beck** has explored 'the risks accompanying goods production (nuclear and chemical mega-technical), genetic research, the threat to the environment, overmilitarization...'. Technological change is not a one way street which generates only the 'pluses' of consumer gadgets and higher material living standards. It also generates 'minuses' of hazardous side effects – the long-term consequences of which are still unclear.

THE PLUSES AND MINUSES OF MODERNISATION

State frontiers provide no defences against the 'dark side' of global modernisation.

> *'Food chains connect practically everyone on earth to everyone else. They dip under borders. The acid content of the air is not only nibbling at sculptures and artistic treasures, it also long ago brought about the disintegration of modern custom barriers.'*
>
> *Beck, 1992*

While risk disadvantage is most acute in the poorest countries a 'boomerang effect' exacts damage on the richest countries as well (for example, the USA has suffered from climate change which may have been caused by its own carbon dioxide emissions). Beck's central theme is that 'we are living in the *age of side effects*...'. Some of these could prove to be lethal: what gives 'historical novelty' to humanity's predicament is 'the possibility of intended and unintended collective suicide...' (Beck, Giddens and Lash, 1994).

A shift takes place in political consciousness

A globalised risk culture changes the way people think and act. In Urry's view, there is a growth in 'radical individualism' which makes it 'harder and harder to sustain oppositional collectivities and collective action'. The result could be the formation of 'a relatively depthless world in which people no longer pursue life-time projects or narratives, and seek short-term advantage in a kind of "calculating hedonism". People's lives are not therefore viewed as the pursuit of ideals, or part of a collective project' (1989). Giddens' more upbeat analysis of the impact of globalisation examined the new possibilities for individual autonomy which have been opened up. There is a heightened sense of reflexivity: instead of passively accepting fate, people deliberately reflect on the life-choices they make and the identities they wish to acquire. Reflexivity is the product of a world that is 'increasingly constituted by information rather than pre-given modes of conduct. It is how we live after the retreat of tradition and nature, because of having to take so many forward-oriented decisions' (Giddens and Pierson 1998).

Study point

Consider the risks that you face most days

1 as a private individual;
2 as a member of a group;
3 as a citizen of your country.

Do any of the risks drive you towards a sense of individuality and do any drive you to look for more commitment to larger groups for security?

New forms of ideological conflict emerge

Time–space compression increases contact between once distant societies. But the more globalisation extends its reach the more likely it is that traditional religious groups will attempt to close themselves off from what are felt to be corrupting and heretical influences. Some religious fundamentalists (such as the 'Televangelists' of the New Christian Right in the USA) now use the media to challenge the secular (non-religious) values that global technology transmits around the planet. For Giddens the key ideological conflict today is between Fundamentalism and Cosmopolitan Reflexivity: 'Refusal of dialogue – an insistence that only one view of the world is possible and that one is already in possession of it – has a particular and potentially destructive significance in a world which precisely depends more and more upon it.' In the view of Samuel Huntingdon the greatest threat to peace now comes from 'The Clash of Civilisations'. He sees the conflict between the West and Islam – 'a different civilisation whose people are convinced of the superiority of their culture and are obsessed with the inferiority of their power' (1998) – as being especially explosive. (In the Islamic view it is the West which seems 'obsessed' with the superiority of its culture and power.)

POINTS OF EVALUATION

1 Globalisation is not a recent development: the compression of time and space has been a centuries' long historical process. The Black Death (bubonic plague), which swept into Europe from Asia between 1348 and 1357 and

destroyed a quarter of its population, shows that a high degree of global interdependency existed long before the arrival of electronics communications. The increase in international trade over the last century has been less spectacular than many globalisation theorists suggest.

2 Globalisation theory both exaggerates the power possessed by the State in the past and the extent to which its power has been depleted and 'hollowed out' in the present. The nation-state continues to be a focal point of cultural identity, retains a monopoly of the legitimate use of force over its territory, and could impose a greater degree of control over financial markets if it chose to do so. Held argues that the powers of the 23 large States which contain 70 per cent of the human race and the 10 states which contain three-quarters of global wealth are still substantial.

'In the short run the collective power of the political authorities representing the three major economic blocks – the USA, the European Union and Japan – remains decisive. This is because most of what happens in every national economy is not directly dependent on what happens in the global economy and transnational operators do not live in cyberspace, but also in the space of real states which control their material infrastructure and the places where they have their often very expensive installations of fixed capital'

Marxism Today, Nov/Dec 1998

---

3 Globalisation theory says little about the question of imperialism – the economic and political domination of less powerful societies by states and transnational corporations (Morgan, 1982). One of the driving forces behind globalisation is the extraction of profit from less developed societies. This important dimension of globalisation is often ignored.

4 Other terms for globalisation could be *McDonaldisation*, *Coco-Colaisation* or *Americanisation*. Rather than being a truly global process it involves the cultural values of one country, the USA, being transmitted to the rest of the world. The USA itself imports very little material from abroad to show on its own media. **George Ritzer** believes that McDonaldisation (managerial and technocratic values of efficiency, predictability, and the standardisation of technology) is a world cultural force. But 'while McDonaldisation *is* a global process' it has 'all the characteristics *rejected* by globalisation theorists – it does have its source in a single nation-state, it does focus on the West in general and the United States in particular, it is connected with the impact of westernisation and Americanisation on the rest of the world, it is attentive to the homogenisation of the world's products and services…' (1996).

Activity

Ritzer's concept of 'McDonaldisation' claims that the principles of the fast food restaurant have 'become a model to be emulated not only by all sorts of businesses, but many other organisations and institutions as well'.

In small groups assess the view that many political organisations – including political parties – are undergoing a process of 'McDonaldisation'.

THE NEW POLITICS OF A MEDIA-SATURATED WORLD

The development of more technologically advanced systems of communication and storage of information brings about political changes. The invention of writing played a key role in the development of ancient civilisations. The invention of printing in the fifteenth century generated massive political upheavals when protesters (Protestants) demanded that the Bible be printed not only in Latin but in their own languages as well. The transmission of the first Morse code message in 1844 marked the arrival of electronic media. Information no longer has to be literally carried from one place to another or physically transcribed on to paper or parchment. The development of cinema and radio before the 1939–45 war, and the emergence of a mass audience for television in the postwar years, changed the ways in which governments and political parties tried to win public support. A global consciousness began to be forged. 'Electric circuitry has overthrown the regime of "time" and "space" and pours upon us instantly and continuously the concerns of all other men. It has reconstituted dialogue on a global scale. Its message is Total Change, ending psychic, social, economic, and political parochialism' (McLuhan and Flore, 1968).

THE POST-MODERNIST INTERPRETATION

Post-modernist theorists believe that:

- The mass production of signs and images by the global media are leading to the creation of a new type of society.
- Baudrillard puts forward the concept of **simulacrum**: images can be so effectively reproduced (or simulated) that it becomes impossible to tell the difference between a copy and an original. Image replaces reality and becomes hyperreality. For Baudrillard modern society is 'puffed up on mere wind' – it is a media creation of invented signs and images.
- In a culture bombarded with market research and opinion polls 'it is no longer necessary that anyone *produce* an opinion, all that is needed is that all *reproduce* public opinion…' (1983).

- **Harvey** (1990) notes that 'corporations, governments, political and intellectual leaders, all value a stable (though dynamic) image as part of their aura of authority and power'.
- Advertising techniques – which are applied to the selling of everything from dog food to Presidents – are 'increasingly geared to manipulating desires and tastes through images that may or may not have anything to do with the product to be sold'.
- Image projection becomes central to both political and personal life. The spirit of our age is summed up by an American image consultant quoted by Harvey: 'Fake it till you make it.'

POINTS OF EVALUATION

1 Empirical (evidence-based) research rejects the claim that electronic media are in fact generating dramatic changes in political consciousness. According to **uses and gratification theory** individuals *use* the media rather than being *used* by it. They read their own biases and prejudices into media material, employ self-censorship (so that programmes and publications which challenge their own opinions are avoided), and 'forget' material which is unsympathetic to their own viewpoints. If media messages fail to win over opinion leaders (individuals who exert influence on others in informal conversations) their impact on the mass of the population will be minimal. What the media do is *reinforce* rather than *change* existing political beliefs.
2 Studies of the effects of party political television broadcasts have found that a process of **selective perception** is at work. Viewers read their own preconceptions and biases into what they see and become *more* convinced of the validity of their own position. They become more informed about party policies – but their voting intentions do not change. The one exception to this general rule is those individuals who have no interest in politics: they *can* be influences by political television. It is on those issues which are marginal and peripheral to readers' and viewers' concerns that the media is most effective in bringing about attitude change.
3 **Cultural effects theorists** see the media as playing an important role in setting the agenda of public debate. They reject the post-modernist claim that political consciousness is being transformed by television, but they accept that the media can 'influence *what people think about* if not *what they think*. Newspaper and television editors make judgements of news priorities; the judgements of one editor influence the views of others; and the result is a media consensus which affects the public's sense of the importance of various issues' (Harrop and Miller, 1987). The media perform a **gatekeeper** function which determines what is (and what is not) 'the' news. Issues are ranked in order of perceived importance (or ignored altogether), The Glasgow University Media Group (GUMG) believes that television news gives an ideologically slanted

interpretation of events which reflects the values and world views of London-based male middle-class journalists and producers. The Media Monitoring Unit, established by the Conservative Party under Lord Tebbit, claimed that the BBC was ideologically biased – but against the right rather than (as GUMG alleged) against the left. **Denver** (1989) writes that the influence of television 'could be long term, slow and subtle – but none the less real'. Social and political change has increased the impact of the media. One factor has been **individuation** – the increased exposure of individuals to the breakdown of communal support (such as the family). Another factor has been partisan dealignment and the weakening of voters' loyalties to political parties.

Activity

In the view of Lord McAlpine, a former treasurer of the Conservative Party, the heroes of the 1992 General Election campaign were 'Sir David English (*Daily Express* editor) and Kelvin McKenzie (*Sun* editor)... Never in the past nine elections have they [the pro-Conservative press] come out so strongly in favour of the Conservatives... This is how the election was won'.

In small groups discuss the validity of Lord McAlpine's view that the result of an election can be determined by a politically biased press.

SOCIAL TRENDS AND POLITICAL INNOVATIONS

Andre Gorz (1982) predicts that technological change will lead to a decline in paid work: 'A society based on mass unemployment is coming into being before our eyes. It consists of a growing mass of the permanently unemployed on one hand, an aristocracy of tenured workers, on the other, and, between them, a proletariat of temporary workers carrying out the least skilled and most unpleasant types of work.' The traditional working class is 'now no more than a privileged minority'. As a force for political change it has been superseded by new social movements which are challenging the work ethic and consumerism.

Will Hutton (1995) argues that 'society is dividing before our eyes, opening up new social fissures in the working population'. A **thirty, thirty, forty** society is being formed. Thirty per cent of the population are *disadvantaged* – they are unemployed or economically inactive (including dependants). Thirty per cent are the *marginalised* and the *insecure* – part-time and casual workers. Forty per cent are the reasonable secure and *privileged* – full-time employees, the self-employed who have held their jobs for over two years, and part-timers who have held their jobs for more than five years. If 'the dynamism of capitalism is to be harnessed to the common good' reforms will have to be introduced which create 'a less unfair,

Study point

On a postcard, tabulate details from the authors listed, make brief summary points of their arguments for revision purposes.

AUTHOR	KEY IDEAS

THE AUTONOMY OF THE INDIVIDUAL

Classical Marxist theorists argue that:

- Political life is shaped by economic factors (such as the mode of production, the level of technology, and the division of society into social classes).
- Location in the class structure shapes individuals' political consciousness.
- Structural forces impose real constraints on action.

In contrast, New Politics theorists emphasise the pivotal role of conscious choice, individual autonomy, and independent action. As a consequence of the growth in electronic media, information technology, and knowledge-based industries:

- The economic 'base' or 'substructure' of society is now shaped by the 'superstructure' of science and media-carried consciousness.
- The class structure has become much more fluid and blurred than in the past and no longer provides a firm foundation for socialists/collectivist politics.
- Today the mass media plays a key role in shaping political consciousness.

Study point

In his *Preface to the Critique of Political Economy* (1859) Karl Marx wrote: 'In the social production of their life, men enter into definite relations that are indispensable and independent of their will, relations of production which correspond to a definite stage of development of their material productive forces. The sum total of these relations of production constitutes the economic structure of society, the real foundation, on which rises a legal and political superstructure and to which correspond definite forms of social consciousness.'

This idea of an *economic base* which determines, supports and conditions a *political superstructure* has had a major influence on sociological theory. In your view, is government policy in the UK shaped by economic factors?

The post-Marxist Interpretation

Barry Hindess and **Paul Hirst** (1977) put forward a 'post-Marxist' analysis of the relationship between economic structure and political action. They reject the view that one can 'read' or predict an individual's politics from his or her class location. The political and the economic operate at two quite different levels. There is no causal linkage between political attitudes and class position, and the one cannot be explained in terms of the other: '... political forces and ideological forms cannot be reduced to the expressions of "interests" determined at the level of economic class relations.' The flaws of classical non-voluntaristic Marxist theory are its class reductionism, economic over-determinism, and failure to recognise the independent dynamism of political ideas.

Jean Baudrillard puts forward a post-modernist analysis of the impact of consumerism, and mass communications. Contemporary society is dominated by a 'sign system' of images: reality is what the media defines it to be. It is through consumer culture that 'our entire society communicates and speaks to and of itself' (quoted by Gane, 1991). Techniques of media manipulation have become more sophisticated and real ideological debate has faded away. Policies are carefully packaged to appeal to mainstream middle-of-the road opinion. Apathy and cynicism about politics increases and the masses save their passions and enthusiasms for expeditions to the shopping malls and surfing the television screens.

Study point

On a postcard, tabulate the authors who present arguments about the autonomy of the individual. Note any key concepts and points which they present.

AUTHORS	KEY CONCEPTS	KEY ARGUMENTS

POINTS OF EVALUATION

1 Eagleton rejects the view that socio-economic location and political consciousness are not closely linked. 'This means, presumably, that it is wholly coincidental that all capitalists are not also revolutionary socialists.' He asks us to imagine ourselves occupying the position of the 'third galley slave from the front of the starboard side' who has to row non-stop for fifteen hours at a stretch. Apart from a few masochists who would actually enjoy such an experience, the more typical response would be for individuals to think hard about how they could extricate themselves from this predicament. There would, in other words, be a fairly close link between individuals' forms of consciousness and their location in the socio-economic structure.

2 Callinicos (1989) describes Baudrillard's analysis as 'a kind of intellectual dandyism' which is not backed by any hard evidence or logical rigour. If reality has been completely transformed into images and hyperreality by the media, how would it be possible for anyone (Baudrillard included) to know what changes in reality have 'really' taken place? The appeal of post-modernist ideas amongst intellectuals in the 1980s and 1990s was the result of two factors: a loss of political confidence and a liking for 'over consumptionist' lifestyles. This 'conjuncture – the prosperity of the Western new middle class combined with the political disillusionment of many of its most articulate members – provides the context to the proliferating talk of post-modernism'.

KEY THEMES IN NEW POLITICS

The *Manifesto for New Times* (1990) focuses on how the political culture has changed in recent decades. Aspects of personal life such as sexuality have been politicised; the idea that the State should play an extensive role in managing society is no longer accepted; the growth of the European Union and the world economy has led to politics becoming increasingly internationalised; old political constituencies (such as the male-dominated labour movement) have fragmented; new sources of collective identity have emerged (such as the greens, ethnicity, and the women's movement); social movements can no longer be neatly fitted into the old left-right political straightjacket.

Kevin Davey notes that contributors to the New Times debate

> 'recognised, and in many cases, celebrated, the numerical decline of the manual working class; the proliferation of cultural identities and the growing importance of choice, consumption and the new communications technologies; the irreversible globalisation of the economy and the appearance of new forms of economic organisation which threatened to make traditional forms of intervention redundant; the marginalisation and possible irrelevance of political parties; the simultaneous rise of the local and the transnational, tending towards the dissolution of nation states; the emergent themes of democratic citizenship, ecology, and feminism and the apparent obsolescence of left/right distinctions in politics.'
>
> 'Waking Up to New Times – Doubts and Dilemmas on the Left' in Perryman, 1994

The concept of New Times was first developed in *Marxism Today*. The October 1988 edition declared:

> 'At the heart of New Times is the shift from the old mass-production Fordist economy to a new, more flexible, post-Fordist order based on computers, information technology and robotics. But New Times are about much more than economic change. Our world is being remade. Mass production, the mass consumer, the big city, big-brother state, the sprawling housing estate, and the nation-state are in decline: flexibility, diversity, differentiation, mobility, communication, decentralisation, and internationalisation are in the ascendant. In the process our own identities, our sense of self, our own subjectivities are being transformed. We are in transition to a new era.'

Stuart Hall (1989) sees 'Post-Fordism' as central to the emergence if New Times. The 'Fordist' era, dominated by the skilled, male, manual working class, factory-based mass production and standardised products, has drawn to a close. Information and electronic-based technologies are transforming the workplace and creating a more specialised and decentralised system of production. Economic life is dominated by global financial markets and multinational companies. The most striking feature of the 'revolution of our times' is its deeply *cultural* character. Issues of 'aesthetics' and 'image' – design, marketing, and style – not only shape economic activity and patterns of consumption but also influence the political process as well. Cultural leadership, the struggle for hegemony, dominates political life. Parties must win the battle for ideas and aspirations if they are to win power.

Dalton and Kuechler (1990) see New Social Movements (NSMs) as changing the political agenda and replacing bureaucratic organisational structures with participatory ones. Post-materialist values are redrawing the landscape of politics: 'Having grown up in a society where security and stability seem relatively assured' many young people aspire to alternative values of 'individual freedom, self-expression and an emphasis on the quality of life'. NSMs 'are a reflection of real threats to global survival. Threats of nuclear devastation and destruction of material resources are no longer the apocalyptic fantasies of a few. They are increasingly perceived as real by the general public. The movements manifest these concerns'.

Geoff Mulgan (1994) argues that the credibility of the political system is being called into question by social and cultural change. He quotes the German theorist Hans Magnus Enzensberger who sees a resemblance between existing political structures and 'repair shops where worried mechanics are bent over stuttering motors and scratch their heads pondering how to make their jalopies work again'. Signs of a transition towards new forms of politics are evident in:

Environmental protestors (such as 'Swampy', shown here) achieved a high media profile in the 1990s.

- A movement in the values of western societies away from traditional authority and the needs of warfare towards self-direction and feminisation.
- The opening up of a huge gap between democracy as an ethos and culture and democracy as a set of institutions (compare public interest in radio phone-ins with public interest in debates in Parliament). Political institutions 'remain stuck in the nineteenth-century form: centralised, pyramidal, national…' Formal politics 'has become a backwater'.
- Since the 1950s the main parties' membership have fallen by more than two-thirds. Today under 5 per cent of their members are aged under 26. Youth 'has largely turned away from orthodox politics towards religion, hedonism and such issues as the environment, animal rights, roads or Aids, but not to the new parties such as the Greens'.
- Globalisation has reduced State power and strengthened local, sectional, and regional identities. The nation is 'in secular retreat'.
- Class divisions have blurred and classes have become less culturally homogeneous (ie more internally divided in terms of life-styles and values). Divisions in the labour market between men and women, skilled and unskilled, insiders and outsiders have intensified. Almost nowhere 'is a class politics now at the leading edge of politics'.

- Confidence in 'universalist ideologies that promised brave new worlds' has faded. People are much more sceptical about the possibility of being able to bring about major changes in the social and economic order and now seek 'change by stealth rather than head-on contest'.
- The contribution the State can make to dealing with macrocosmic issues (such as the spread of Aids and global warming) and microcosmic issues (such as identity, sexuality and home life) is very limited. Such issues 'are soluble less through the passing of laws and decrees than through changes of culture and behaviour'. People have been disappointed by the problem-solving skills of government and interest in politics has declined as a result.
- Politics has made an 'uneasy adaptation' to the era of electronic communications. 'The founding ideas of modern politics were high moments of print culture: the linear argument of the constitution, the manifesto and the programme.' Shifts in media forms 'are now accelerating far ahead of the ability of political institutions to keep up ...'. Generations brought up on computer games 'will make much stronger demands on politics to deliver what they get elsewhere: not just the monologues of twentieth-century politics, but rather a politics that is much more personal, confessional and interrogative'.
- The new politics will involve 'a shift towards electronic forms of decision-making' and a 'greater mix of formal representative structures and direct democracy, through referenda and polls'.
- 'The tectonic plates of politics are on the move, forced by deeper pressures of technology, social organisation and values. We should be prepared for a few earthquakes.'

Paul Hirst (1994) describes the present era as one in which 'the old certainties of politics have dissolved, in which politics and society are more pluralistic and less capable of being dragooned by the ideological programmes of left and right.' Economic issues of property distribution no longer dominate political life. 'There are new types of nationalist and regional autonomist parties, and ethnic and religiously-based campaigns. There are also new forms of politics centred on resistance to racism, gender issues, the environmental question and on lifestyles.'

Anthony Giddens (1991) distinguishes between **emancipatory politics** and **life politics**. The central focus of emancipatory politics is on life-chances: 'the reduction or elimination of exploitation, inequality or oppression. The central focus of life politics is on life decisions: the choices individuals make, the kind of risks they take, the identities they seek to acquire. Tradition no longer assigns scripts for life: in a rapidly changing world people have to learn to be their own script writers. Existential questions of choice, self-discovery and identity now encroach on the political terrain.

Shaun Best (1997) has analysed the concept of postmodern politics in *The Social Science Teacher*.

- Political uncertainty forms part of the postmodern condition: 'we feel as if the *social* is dissolving.'
- There is no coherent moral code which binds people together. '... this means that morally *anything goes*; this is what theorists call the *aesthetisation of life*.'
- Individuals have lost faith in what Jean-Francois Lyotard called **metanarratives** – 'belief systems which we all once accepted and which gave us reassurance.' (Lyotard defines postmodernism as 'incredulity towards metanarratives'.)
- The decline of metanarratives (or grand narratives) means there is a greater emphasis on human agents actively making autonomous choices and not being pushed this way and that by forces they cannot control: 'the *postmodern political ethos* is therefore democratic in nature.
- In postmodern politics single issue campaigns and New Social Movements come to the fore. Political parties and class-based movements become less relevant. The State is no longer regarded as the primary focus of political activity. The rigid barriers between political and private life are dismantled, and politics is 'decentered' towards the 'micro' sphere of the self and personal identity.

Study point

On a postcard make a note of the key authors listed in the text and note any concepts and important arguments they make.

AUTHORS	KEY CONCEPTS	KEY ARGUMENTS

Study point

Keynote articles from *The Social Science Teacher* – plus access to other sociological websites – are available on the Association for the Teaching of the Social Sciences website:

http://www.le.ac.uk/education/centres/ATSS/atss.html

THE NEW POLITICS AND THE OLD POLITICS

Table 9: *A comparison of the New Politics and the Old Politics*

THE NEW POLITICS	THE OLD POLITICS
Globalisation injects an international dimension into political debate	The political agenda is normally dominated by national/domestic issues
Decentralised and non-institutionalised New Social Movements play a key role	Old Social Movements with formal structures play a key role
High level of participation in single issue campaigns ('sub-politics')	High level of participation in political parties
Class divisions no longer dominate politics	Class divisions have a major influence on politics
Growing scepticism towards ideologies and grand narratives	Ideologies and grand narratives exert a powerful influence on political life
Public confidence in the problem-solving powers of the State declines	The State is seen as a key lever of social and political change
The electronic media play a central role in political communication	Print culture plays a central role in political communication
High levels of interactivity between government and the governed	Low levels of interactivity between government and governed
Increasing use of referenda, opinion polls, focus groups, and electronic technology	Traditional representative democracy is based almost exclusively on elections
Concept of the 'political' extended to include micro-issues of identity and relationships	Concept of the 'political' is largely confined to macro-issues of public policy
Political debate reflects the concerns of a culturally diverse and pluralistic society	Political debate assumes that society is culturally homogeneous and uniform
The division between Left and Right declines in significance and a 'Third Way' is sought	The division between Left and Right dominates political debate
Growth in reflexivity leads to demands for greater political participation – individuals are defined as 'citizens'	The political culture encourages individuals to accept passive political roles – individuals are defined as 'subjects'
Life politics issues become part of mainstream political debate	Life politics issues are largely ignored in political debate
The 'New Individualism' has a major influence on politics	Collectivism has a major influence on politics

SUMMARY

- Globalisation has been defined as 'action at distance': developments in communications and transportation have radically reduced the constraints of geography.
- Globalisation has been accompanied by a decline in the power of the nation-state, the emergence of a risk culture, and a shift in consciousness towards greater reflexivity.
- Cultural domination (McDonaldisation) is one of the features of globalisation.
- Globalisation is accompanied by a growth in fundamentalist ideologies. A new global consciousness is being formed.
- Uses and gratification theory rejects the post-modernist view that the mass media are having a dramatic impact on political consciousness.
- Cultural effects theory sees the mass media as setting the agenda of public debate and having a significant influence on political thinking.
- Social and technological trends are generating new inequalities (such as the 'thirty, thirty, forty society') as well as opening up new possibilities for democratic debate and interaction between government and governed.
- New Politics theorists see the 'superstructure' of knowledge and ideas as having a key influence on society.
- 'New Times' theorists believe that cultural forces will play a pivotal role in the twenty-first century. Our fragmented consumer-oriented society is very different from the one based on 'smokestack' proletarian Fordist industries.
- Issues of class, property, and the State were central to the agenda of the 'Old Politics'. Issues of identity, lifestyle, and the environment are central to the agenda of the 'New Politics'. Metanarratives have been displayed by life politics.

POINTS OF EVALUATION

1. The view that economic factors (the 'base' or substructure) shape politics and ideology (the 'superstructure') is rejected by New Politics theorists. Yet many of the cultural changes they describe are the direct result of economic factors (eg rising material living standards, electronic communications, information technology, and automation). The 'base' continues to generate social and political change.
2. New Politics theorists claim that the influence exerted by social class on politics is in decline. But globalisation has intensified inequalities of power and wealth. A collapse of the global economy could lead to a resurgence in the very class-based ideological conflicts which have been dismissed as 'Old Politics'.

3 New Politics theorists have their own ideological agenda. They approve of the goals of feminist, ecological, and anti-nuclear New Social Movements and exaggerate their significance. But 'new' social movements which have populist and neo-fascist goals tend to be ignored.
4 The 'New Politics' does not signify an end of metanarratives. It is simply a new form of metanarrative – one which meets the concerns of the individualistic self in a global consumer culture.

Group work

1 Monitor local newspapers for a week. Make a list of economic, cultural and political developments in your locality which have been influenced by global factors. Divide into small groups and collate information. Each group then presents a summary of the leading global influences which are at work in your locality.
2 Undertake a short joint project. Group members to establish:
- the number of New Social Movements with members in your area
- their policies, strategies of influence, membership size and composition
- the views of a sample of the public on their activities and objectives.

Key Concepts Activity

Write a short definition of the following concepts: globalisation; reflexivity; manufactured risks; the media's gatekeeper function; Post-Fordism; the 'thirty, thirty, forty society'; metanarratives; emancipatory politics; life politics.

Practice Questions

1 'The power of the nation-state has been "hollowed out" by the forces of globalisation.' Explain and discuss.
2 New Social Movements are said to be radically different from Old Social Movements. How valid is this claim?

Coursework

1 New Politics theorists are critical of existing forms of representative democracy and advocate the use of more 'interactive' forms of communication (such as electronic polling and referendums, use of the Internet, citizens' juries). Conduct interviews with a random sample of the public to find out whether they favour the introduction of new forms of communication between government and the governed.

2 New Politics theorists claim that the 'Old Politics' was dominated by 'materialist values' and that young people subscribe to a new political agenda based on 'post-materialist' values. Interview individuals from different age groups to find out:

- whether support for 'post-materialist' values is more widespread amongst the young than the old;
- whether a significant proportion of young people support 'post-materialist' values.

FURTHER READING

THE SOCIOLOGY OF POWER

Baudrillard, J. (1987) *Forget Foucault*, Semiotext(e).
Dahl, R. A. (1961) *Who Governs?*, Yale University Press.
Grant, W. (1989) *Pressure Groups, Politics and Democracy in Britain*, Philip Allan.
Hewitt, C. J. (1974) 'Elites and the Distribution of Power in British Society' in Stanworth, P. and Giddens, A. (editors) *Elites and Power in British Society*, CUP.
Lukes, S (1974) *Power: A Radical View*, Macmillan.
Mann, M. (1986) *The Sources of Social Power, Volume 1*, Cambridge.
Mann, M. (1993) *The Sources of Social Power, Volume 11*, Cambridge.
Miliband, R. (1969) *The State in Capitalist Society*, Weidenfeld & Nicolson.
Mills, C. W. (1967) *Power, Politics And People*, OUP.
Poulantzas, N. (1978) *Classes in Contemporary Capitalism*, Verso.
Rabinow, P. (editor) (1986) *The Foucault Reader*, Penguin.
Rose, A. M. (1967) *The Power Structure: Political Process in American Society*, OUP.
Scott, J. (1991) *Who Rules Britain?*, Polity.
Worsley, P. (1977) *Introducing Sociology*, Penguin.

THE STATE AND DEMOCRACY

de Ste. Croix, G. E. M. (1981) *The Class Struggle in the Ancient Greek World*, Duckworth.
Djilas, M. (1957) *The New Class. An Analysis of the Communist System*, Thames & Hudson.
Goodwin, B. (1997) *Using Political Ideas*, John Wiley.
Jary, D. & Jary, J. (1995) *Collins Dictionary of Sociology* (second edition), HarperCollins.
Leys, C. (1986) *Politics in Britain. An Introduction*, Verso.
Marcuse, H. (1964) *One Dimensional Man*, Routledge & Kegan Paul.
McCelland, J. S. (1996) *A History Of Western Political Thought*, Routledge.
McLean, I. (editor) (1996) *The Concise Oxford Dictionary of Politics*, Oxford.
Mills, C. W. (1956), *The Power Elite*, OUP.
Moore, B. J. (1967) *Social Origins of Dictatorship and Democracy. Lord and Peasant in the Making of the Modern World*, Penguin.
Offe, C. (1984) *Contradictions of the Welfare State*, Hutchinson.
Scruton, R. (1983) *A Dictionary of Political Thought*, Macmillan.
Therborn, G. (1978) *What Does The Ruling Class Do When It Rules?*, Verso.

IDEOLOGIES

Abercrombie, N., Hill, N., Turner, B. S. (1980) *The Dominant Ideology Thesis*, Allen & Unwin.
Birch, A. H. (1998) *The British System of Government*, Routledge.

Bullock, A., and Stallybrass, O. (editors) (1977) *The Fontana Dictionary of Modern Thought*, Fontana.
Coates, D. (1980) *Labour in Power? A Study of the Labour Government 1974–1979*, Longman.
Eagleton, T. (1991) *Ideology. An Introduction*, Verso.
Eccleshall, R., Geoghegan, V., and Wilford, R. (1984) *Political Ideologies*, Routledge.
Etzioni, A. (1993) *The Spirit of Community. The Reinvention of American Society*, Simon & Schuster.
Fukuyama, F. (1992) *The End Of History And The Last Man*, Penguin.
Giddens, A. (1994) *Beyond Left and Right. The Future of Radical Politics*, Polity.
Giddens, A. (1998) *The Third Way: The Renewal of Social Democracy*, Polity.
Hutchinson, J., and Smith, A. D. (editors) (1994) *Nationalism*, Oxford.
Kitchen, M. (1976) *Fascism*, Macmillan.
Leach, R. (1991) *British Political Ideologies*, Philip Allan.
Lent, A. (editor) (1998) *New Political Thought. An Introduction*, Lawrence & Wishart.
Lukes, S. (1973) *Emile Durkheim. His Life and Work: A Historical and Critical Study*, Penguin.
Plamenatz, J. (1970) *Ideology*, Pall Mall.
Willetts, D. (1992) *Modern Conservatism*, Penguin.
Woolf, S. J. (editor) (1968) *European Fascism*, Weidenfeld & Nicolson.

Pressure Groups and Public Policy

Abercrombie, N., and Warde, A. (1994) *Contemporary British Society. A New Introduction to Sociology*, Polity.
Baggott, R. (1995) *Pressure Group Politics*, Manchester University Press.
Barrett, M. (1980) *Women's Oppression Today. Problems in Marxist Feminist Analysis*, Verso.
Barrett, M. and Philips, A. (editors) (1992) *Destabilizing Theory. Contemporary Feminist Debates*, Polity.
Coates, D. (1994) *The Question of UK Decline. State, Society and Economy*, Harvester Wheatsheaf.
Dahl, R. A. (1989) *Democracy and Its Critics*, Yale.
Grant, W. (1989) *Pressure Groups, Politics and Democracy in Britain*, Philip Allan.
Hoad, D. (Spring 1998) 'Direct Action and the Environment Movement', *Talking Politics*.
Jones, B. (editor) (1994) *Politics UK*, Harvester Wheatsheaf.
Jordan, G. and Maloney, W. (1997) *The Protest Business? Mobilizing campaign groups*, Manchester University.
Kingdom, J. (1991) *Government and Politics in Britain*, Polity.
McKenzie, R. T. (1963) *British Political Parties*, Heinemann.
Roberts, D. (editor) (1995) *British Politics in Focus*, Causeway.

POLITICAL PARTICIPATION AND VOTING BEHAVIOUR

Butler, D., and Stokes, D. (1974) *Political Change In Britain*, Macmillan.
Butler, D. and Kavanagh, D. (1997) *The British General Election of 1997*, Macmillan.
Crewe, I. (1993) 'Parties and Electors' in Budge, I., and McKay., D. (editors) *The Developing British Political System: the 1990s*, 3rd Edition, Longman.
Crouch, C. (1990) 'Industrial Relations' in Dunleavy, P. (editor) (1990) *Developments in British Politics 3*, Macmillan.
Denver, D. (1989) *Elections and Voting Behaviour in Britain*, Philip Allan.
Downs, A. (1957) *An Economic Theory of Democracy*, Harper and Row.
Dunleavy, P. (editor) (1997) *Developments in British Politics 5*, Macmillan.
Dunleavy, P., and Husbands, C. (1985) *British Democracy at the Crossroads*, Longman.
Giddens, A. (1997) *Sociology*, 3rd Edition, Polity.
Harrop, M., and Miller, W. L. (1987) *Elections and Voters. A Comparative Introduction*, Macmillan.
Heath, A., Jowell, R., and Curtice, J. (1985) *How Britain Votes*, Pergamon.
Hill, C. (1970) *God's Englishman. Oliver Cromwell and the English Revolution*, Weidenfeld and Nicolson.
Himmelweit, H., Humphreys, P., and Jaeger, M. (1985) *How Voters Decide*, Open University Press.
Marshall, G. et al (1988) *Social Class in Modern Britain*, Hutchinson.
McKenzie, R. T., and Silver, A. (1968) *Angels in Marble*, Heinemann.
Parkin, F. (1968) *Middle-Class Radicalism*, Manchester University Press.
Parry, G., Moyser, G., and Day, N., (1991) *Political Participation in Britain*, Cambridge.
Rose, R., and McAllister, I. (1990) *The Loyalties of Voters. A Lifetime Learning Model*, Sage.
Sennett, R. (1974) *The Fall of Public Man*, Faber and Faber.
Whiteley, P., Seyd, P., and Richardson, J. (1994) *True Blues. The Politics of Conservative Party Membership*, Clarendon Press.

GLOBALISATION AND THE NEW POLITICS

Baudrillard, J. (1983) *Simulations*, Semiotext(e).
Bauman, Z. (1998) *Globalization. The Human Consequences*, Polity.
Beck, U. (1992) *Risk Society*, Sage.
Beck, U., Giddens, A., and Lash, S. (1994) *Reflexive Modernization. Politics. Tradition and Aesthetics in Modern Social Order*, Polity.
Best, S. (1997) 'Postmodern Politics', *Social Science Teacher*, Summer 1997.
Callinicos, A. (1989) *Against Postmodernism. A Marxist Critique*, Polity.

Dalton, R. J., and Kuechler, M. (1990) *Challenges to Political Order. New Social and Political Movements in Western Democracies*, Polity.

Gane. M. (1991) *Baudrillard's Bestiary. Baudrillard and Culture*, Routledge.

Giddens, A. (1991) *Modernity and Self-Identity. Self and Society in the Late Modern Age*, Polity.

Giddens, A. (1994) *Beyond Left and Right. The Future of Radical Politics*, Polity.

Giddens, A. and Pierson, C. (1998) *Conversations With Anthony Giddens. Making Sense of Modernity*, Polity.

Goodhart, R and Tyrell, D. (October 1998) 'Opinion Poll Democracy', *Prospect*.

Gorz, A. (1982) *Farewell to the Working Class. An Essay on Post-Industrial Socialism*, Pluto.

Hall, S. and Jacques, M. (editors) (1989) *New Times. The Changing Face of Politics in the 1990s*, Lawrence & Wishart.

Harvey, D. (1990) *The Condition of Postmodernity. An Enquiry into the Origins of Cultural Change*, Blackwell.

Hindess, B. and Hirst, P. (1977) *Mode of Production and Social Formation*, Macmillan.

Hirst, P. (1994) *Associative Democracy. New Forms of Economic and Social Governance*, Polity.

Huntingdon, S. P. (1998) *The Clash of Civilisations and the Remarking of World Order*, Simon & Schuster.

Hutton, W. (1995) *The State We're In*, Jonathan Cape.

Hutton, W. (1997) *The State To Come*, Vintage.

Lasch, C. (1995) *The Revolt of the Elites*, Norton.

Lash, A. and Urry, J. (1994) *Economies of Signs and Space*, Sage.

McLuhan, M. and Fiore, Q. (1968) *The Medium is the Message*, Allen Lane.

Morgan, I. (Autumn 1982) 'Theories of Imperialism: a bibliographical sketch' in *Journal of Area Studies*.

Mulgan, G. (15.4.94) 'Party-free politics', *New Statesman & Society*.

Perri 6 (1997) *Holistic government*, Demos.

Perryman, M. (1994) *Altered States. Postmodernism, Politics, Culture*, Lawrence & Wishart.

Ritzer, G. (1996) *The McDonaldisation of Society*, Pine Forge Press.

Robertson, R. (1992) *Globalisation*, Sage.

Smart, B. (1993) *Postmodernity*, Routledge.

Soja, E. W. (1989) *Postmodern Geographies. The Reassertion of Space in Critical Social Theory*, Verso.

Urry, J. (1989) 'The End of Organised Capitalism' in Hall, S. and Jacques, M. (editors) *New Times. The Changing Face of Politics in the 1990s*, Lawrence & Wishart.

Walters, M. (1995) *Globalisation*, Routledge.

ANSWERS

CHAPTER 2 ANSWERS TO STUDY POINT PAGE 18

1 Elitist, from: *Power, Politics and People. The Collected Essays of C. Wright Mills*, edited by I. L. Horowitze (1967)
2 Marxist, from W. L. Guttsman, *The British Political Elite* (1968)
3 Pluralist, from Robert A. Dahl, *Who Governs?* (1961)

CHAPTER 3 ANSWERS TO STUDY POINT PAGES 30 AND 32

1 Corporate from: Colin Leys, *Politics in Britain. An Introduction* (1986)
2 New Class from: Roger Scruton, *A Dictionary of Political Thought* (1982)
3 Power Elitist from: D. and J. Jary (editors), *Collins Dictionary of Sociology* (1995)
4 Totalitarian from: Iain McLean (editor), *The Concise Oxford Dictionary of Politics* (1996)
5 Pluralist from: D. and J. Jary (editors), *Collins Dictionary of Sociology* (1995)
6 Capitalist from: Goran Therborn, *What Does The Ruling Class Do When It Rules?* (1978)

CHAPTER 4 ANSWERS TO STUDY POINT PAGES 59 AND 60

1 Liberalism from: John Stuart Mill, *On Liberty* (1859)
2 Conservatism from: Roger Scruton, *A Dictionary of Political Thought* (1983)
3 Fascism from Benito Mussolini, *The Doctrine of Fascism* (1933)
4 Nationalism from: John Armstrong, *Nations Before Nationalism* (1982)
5 Socialism from: Lord Douglas Jay, quoted in 'The Labour Party and Socialism' by I. Morgan, *Politics Review*, November (1995)
6 Communism from: *The Concise Oxford Dictionary of Sociology*, edited by Gordon Marshall (1994)
7 Green ideology from: Robert Leach, *British Political Ideologies* (1991)

CHAPTER 5 ANSWERS TO STUDY POINT ON PAGE 76

1 is an ideological outsider group
2 is a think-tank (founded in 1884)
3 is a peak group
4 is a protective group
5 is a think-tank (founded in 1988)
6 is a promotional group
7 is a think-tank (founded in 1993).

CHAPTER 6 ANSWERS TO STUDY POINT ON PAGE 93

Postwar British Prime Ministers

- Attlee: Labour
- Churchill: Conservative
- Eden: Conservative
- Macmillan: Conservative
- Douglas-Home: Conservative
- Wilson: Labour
- Heath: Conservative
- Callaghan: Labour
- Thatcher: Conservative
- Major: Conservative
- Blair: Labour

GLOSSARY

Authority institutionalised and legitimate power which rests upon consent.

Autocracy the dictatorial and arbitrary exercise of power by a single ruler or ruling group.

Coercive Power the exercise of power by the use of force and violence.

Collective Power power to achieve shared goals by groups which co-operate and work together.

Consensus agreement on key political goals and values.

Convergence Theory industrial societies come to resemble each other.

Corporate State key functional groups (or corporations) are incorporated into the decision-making process of the state.

Distributive Power a group gains sectional advantage and increases its power at the expense of another group.

Emancipatory Politics aims to free individuals from inequality and injustice and enhance their life-chances.

Embourgeoisement the acceptance of middle class (or bourgeois) attitudes, values and beliefs.

Executive government and state institutions which execute and implement policy.

Fordism assemble line-style production of standardised goods for a mass market.

Globalisation the shrinking of time and space and the emergence of a world economy and a planet-wide network of transport and communications.

Glocalisation interaction between the global and the local.

Government the part of the executive which formulates public policy and takes key political decisions.

Hegemony cultural and ideological leadership exercised by a dominant class or group.

Ideological State Apparatus institutions controlled by the state (such as the mass media and schools) which support the dominant ideology.

Inducive Power the exercise of power over others by the offer of rewards and incentives.

Judiciary judges and courts of law.

Legislature a law-making assembly or Parliament.

Life Politics the politics of personal identity and self-actualisation.

Manufactured Risks dangers to life generated by technological change.

Macro-Physics of Power the study of the power exerted by large-scale institutions such as the state.

Media Gatekeepers individuals (such as newspaper editors and television producers) who control and regulate the flow of news and information.

Metanarratives total explanations (or grand theories) of the meaning of History and the nature of Truth.

Micro-Physics of Power the study of power relationships in everyday life.

Multiple-Elite Theory numerous elites (groups with authority and status) shape and influence the decision-making process.

Oligarchy power and decision-making is concentrated in the hands of the few.

Pluralism a plurality (numerous) groups have access to power and influence over the decision-making process.

Post-Fordism flexible production for specialised markets made possible by development in robotics and information technology.

Post-Modernism metanarratives which claim to know 'The Truth' are no longer seen as credible or believable.

Psephology the study of voting behaviour.

Rational Choice Theory the analysis of politics in terms of individuals who seek to maximise their own economic self-interest.

Reflexivity the capacity to reflect on the consequences of action and change one's self.

Repressive State Apparatus institutions controlled by the state (such as the police and the military) which use force and violence to defend the established political order.

Ruling Class owners of the means of production and large-scale capital who are able to exercise a decisive degree of political power.

Separation of Powers control over the executive, the legislature and the judiciary is in the hands of different individuals and is not concentrated in the hands of a single group.

Simulacrum a reality-defining media image or copy of an image which shapes consciousness.

State a set of permanent and authoritative institutions which hold a monopoly of the legitimate use of force over a given territory.

Totalitarian State a one party-state which uses modern technology to impose total control over the population.